With Wellington's Staff at Waterloo

COLONEL BASIL JACKSON

With Wellington's Staff at Waterloo

The reminiscences of a staff officer
during the Campaign of 1815 and
with Napoleon on St.Helena

Basil Jackson

LEONAUR

With Wellington's Staff at Waterloo
The reminiscences of a staff officer
during the Campaign of 1815 and
with Napoleon on St. Helena
by Basil Jackson

First published under the title
Notes and Reminiscences of a Staff Officer

Leonaur is an imprint
of Oakpast Ltd

ISBN: 978-0-85706-172-0(hardcover)
ISBN: 978-0-85706-171-3 (softcover)

http://www.leonaur.com

Publisher's Notes

Contents

Introduction

These *Notes and Reminiscences* were printed for private circulation in 1877, the author not thinking that they were of sufficient interest to justify publication. The reader will probably be of a different opinion. They are now published by the kind permission of Mrs Simcoe, of Wolford, Devon, the author's daughter.

Lieutenant-Colonel Basil Jackson died in October 1889, at the advanced age of ninety-four. His death was noticed in the *Times* and other papers of the day, the former referring to him as "one of the four surviving heroes of Waterloo." The other three at that time were the Earl of Albemarle, General Whichcote, and Lieutenant-Colonel Hewitt.

It is certain that Colonel Jackson rendered essential service in the Waterloo Campaign. For instance, he mentions having made, on the instructions of Sir Hudson Lowe, a special report of the route by which the Prussians retired after Ligny. This report was transmitted to General Gneisenau and undoubtedly helped to form his speedy decision to retreat northward by a by-road to Wavre immediately after the defeat.

It has been stated—apparently with a view to detract from the weight of Colonel Jackson's testimony in favour of Sir Hudson Lowe—that the latter's younger son, Major-General Edward William De Lancy Lowe, married a daughter of Colonel Jackson, and in the notice of Major-General Lowe in the *Dictionary of National Biography* this statement is repeated. It is, however, a pure fabrication. I have the authority both of Mrs Simcoe and of Miss Lowe for saying that Major-General Lowe never even met the lady in question.

I have added in square brackets a few footnotes where they seemed desirable, by way of giving additional information. In the preparation of these notes I have to thank my friend Dr J. H. Rose—the author of the well-known *Life of Napoleon I.*—for much valuable assistance. I also acknowledge the courtesy of Dr J. F. W. Silk in allowing me to reproduce the sketch of Napoleon and views of St Helena from his admirable collection. The portrait of Colonel Jackson is from a photograph, taken a year before his death, by Messrs Busten of Ross.

R. C. S.

Preface

I venture to inscribe this little volume to a fair friend, who, after perusing it in manuscript, not only gave it commendation, but was induced to transfer to canvas one of the Waterloo scenes therein described.

Before dawn of the morn after the battle, when on my way to the army with the Duke's order for it to march, I paused for a few minutes at the little farm of La Haye Sainte (around which there had been fierce struggles), to survey the scene before me.

This was the time chosen for the picture, which is painted, I presume to think, very skilfully and correctly, as to the run of the ground, and the touching—nay, appalling—appearance of its *still* occupants, which, but a few hours before, were valiant men and noble horses!

Several friends who have read my manuscript have urged me to publish; but "there is a time for all things;" and possibly, had it been in existence sixty years ago, when the book trade reaped an abundant harvest from the field of Waterloo, it might have answered a publisher's purpose to bring it out. But when many years have been suffered to pass by, and when we only hear of Waterloo as a bridge, a place, or a road, it was far too late. Some portion of my *Recollections* did appear in the *United Service Magazine*,[1] about thirty years back, which I deemed sufficient.

About St Helena, my few readers will probably feel interested, as I was a good deal behind the scenes in the drama enacted there, as they will find on perusal.

Ross, August 1877.

---

1. October and November 1843, and March 1844.

CHAPTER 1

The Royal Staff Corps

In September 1808, in my thirteenth year, I entered the Military College, and, having completed the prescribed course of instruction when not quite sixteen, was appointed ensign in a line regiment; but, in order to enable me further to prosecute my studies, permission was given me to pass six months more at the College. Meanwhile, the Governor was so good as to recommend my being transferred from the 26th Regiment to the Royal Staff Corps, a superior service, the officers of which were expected to be acquainted with the duties of the Quarter-master-General's Department, together with those of civil engineers; the sergeants and rank and file being chiefly artisans, having some trade of a kind to be useful with an army in the field.

Although not quite perfection, the Military College, in my day, was an admirable school of discipline, as well as education generally, and I have always felt thankful for the training I there received. In my humble opinion, a great mistake was made in changing it from a school for boys to one of candidates for the army, between the ages of eighteen and twenty-one; thus obtaining, what Lord Hardinge, the then Secretary for War, characterised as the "readymade article." The plan has worked very badly, as may well be supposed, and will, I doubt not, in process of time, compel a return to the original system.

I joined the headquarters of my corps at Hythe, in January 1812, and nothing worth recording happened to me till towards the end of 1813, when the general rising of nations against Napoleon induced our Government to send a small force to Holland to encourage the rise of the Dutch; and, not a little to my surprise and gratification, I had the good fortune to be specially appointed to serve in the expedition, on the staff of the quartermaster-general. The force in question was between 6000 and 7000 men. We were, I believe, of some use

11

in keeping the French garrisons of Antwerp, Bergen-op-Zoom, and other fortresses, within their walls.

To recount our marches and counter-marches, through the snows of the terribly severe winter of 1813-14, would be of little interest to the reader; neither would our failure to damage the French men-of-war ensconced in the basin of Antwerp, by means of shells and Congreve rockets, nor our abortive and disastrous endeavour to take the strong fortress of Bergen-op-Zoom by surprise, be of much interest at the present day. However, our proceedings were very useful to me, as giving me experience, and enabling me gradually to acquire some knowledge of my duties as a staff officer, in which, at starting, I was, as a mere boy, anything but competent.

In the early spring of 1814, the fortresses we were employed in watching, together with the territory of Holland and Belgium, were evacuated by the enemy. The division of the army to which I was attached marched into Antwerp, while our headquarters were established at Brussels; our gallant old commander, Sir Thomas Graham, there resigned his command to the hereditary Prince of Orange, who held the rank of general in the British Service; and our force, which at that time may have numbered 10.000 men, was distributed over the Belgic territory, where it lay cantoned, and eventually formed the nucleus of the army of Waterloo.

One of my first duties, when attached to our headquarters at Brussels, was to visit many of the principal towns in Belgium, and ascertain what barrack accommodation they afforded for our troops; my tour comprised Dendermond, Ghent, Bruges, Ath, Tournay, Mons, etc.; in some of those I found that old monasteries had been converted into this useful purpose, being of great extent, and in most respects suitable. When at Tournay, feeling curiosity to see the great fortress of Lille, I went thither—an imprudent step, as it contained a large French garrison, not well disposed towards us redcoats. However, I was enabled to walk round the ramparts, dined at a restaurant, and regained Tournay without meeting with anything unpleasant. This trip gave me an extensive knowledge of a large portion of the country, which was useful to me afterwards.

About this time Sir Hudson Lowe was appointed quartermaster-general, succeeding colonel, afterwards Earl, Cathcart, who was much liked by his subordinates, and whom we saw depart with regret. His successor, however, proved to be all we could desire, as an active, diligent, and accomplished officer, who not only worked hard himself, but also kept his officers on the alert, evincing towards them at the same time the utmost consideration. He was desirous of obtaining information about the highways and byways of the country, and kept me a good deal upon the trot; and I remember making a special report on the route by which the Prussians retired after the battle of Ligny. Sir Hudson remained with us until a few weeks before the Waterloo Campaign opened, when he was given a command in the Mediterranean, his force occupying Toulon and Marseilles.

When Blücher's headquarters became established at Liège, several of his generals visited Brussels, and were hospitably entertained by Sir Hudson Lowe, their old companion-in-arms, he having been our military *attaché* with the army of Silesia. Having no *aide-de-camp*, he generally invited me to act as such when entertaining the Prussian officers, and I felt greatly interested in hearing them talk over the incidents of their memorable campaigns, terminating in the occupation of Paris by the Allies. The conversation was always in the French language, Sir Hudson not being sufficiently versed in German to speak it with ease.

Brussels was exceedingly gay at this period as the residence of the newly-made King, and headquarters of our troops, the *élite* of whom were lodged in the city; then families flocked in from home, all tending to render the place alive. Reviews of the troops often occurred, taking place in the park whenever any great personage came. Then we had races, fox-hunting, and cricket, all of which were patronised by the Prince. The hunting, however, was a great failure; in the first place the Belgian foxes had no idea that they were to run before the hounds, not being trained, I presume, to do so from their birth like our own; moreover, the farmers could not see the propriety of our riding over their land: indeed, the Prince had to pay a considerable sum as indemnification for alleged injury to the crops. This drove us to hunt in the forest of Soignies, but, as the stupid foxes would not run, hunting had to be given up.

CHAPTER 2

Brussels

Louis XVIII. being now comfortably seated at the Tuileries, and tranquilly reigning throughout France, the allied forces withdrew from Paris, several bodies of Prussians passing through Brussels on their way to Germany, They were composed of hardy, rough-looking men, with well-worn *habiliments*. Some females marched with them, sitting astride, and looking as warlike as the soldiers. The artillery was not imposing in the eye of an Englishman, accustomed to see our magnificent display in that arm.

Bodies of French soldiers also passed through the city, composed chiefly of prisoners captured during the disastrous retreat from Moscow, two years before—a mere dirty, ragged mob. Who could believe that those poor hobbling, shabby creatures had formed part of the finest, best appointed, and most numerous army of modern days? But one small detachment appeared in very different guise: it was preceded by four small field guns, and the soldiers had arms and well-filled knapsacks; this was the garrison of some fort in North Holland, which, having held the place till hostilities ceased, had marched homewards with all the honours of war. The men had the proud and martial port of the French imperial soldiers, their countenances wearing nothing of the scowl of the released prisoners I have mentioned. Thus were many thousands of trained and seasoned warriors returned to France, ready, aye and eager, to range themselves under the eagles when Napoleon surprised the world by landing in France from Elba.

The English families rendered Brussels very gay, and I must say that my countrywomen contrasted most favourably with the Belgian ladies, exciting indeed the admiration of the Brussels gentlemen. "*Il faut avouer que le sexe est beau en Angleterre,*" was an exclamation I heard more than once; and certainly we had several fine specimens of British beauty. There were frequent balls in the magnificent room called the *Concert Noble*, where the *élite* of both natives and foreigners assembled to display their charms to the best advantage; but the latter far eclipsed their rivals. The dances were waltzes, quadrilles, and occasionally a *colonne*, or what we call a country dance. I must say that, in dancing, the English, both male and female, had to yield the palm to the *Bruxellois*. However, not liking to be outdone, even in dancing, many of our officers took lessons, and in time were able to make at least a respectable appearance, both in the quadrille and waltz.

Of course there were flirtations, which meant nothing, but the young ladies of the place had got a notion into their silly heads that Englishmen were prone to *enlèvements*, and I had good reason for thinking that some of our young waltzing *belles* felt disappointed that no *enlèvement* took place. In the winter of 1814-15 there was snow enough for sledge-driving, and gay parties were formed to enjoy an amusement so novel to most of us. We had, too, Court receptions, such as *levées* and drawing-rooms; and I was present when Lord Castlereagh invested the King of the Netherlands with the Order of the Garter—an imposing ceremony.

Thus were we amusing ourselves, when a rumour came that Napoleon was again in France; but for a day or two it was thought to be only an idle *shave*;[1] we were, however, soon undeceived, and thought that in all probability we should soon see him in Belgium. Accordingly, there was a universal bustle of preparation; the spade and the pick-axe were set to work to repair and strengthen the frontier fortresses of Mons and Tournay; and soon troops of all arms began to reach Ostend, our Home Government fully appreciating the call for vigorous and prompt action. But we hailed with joy the arrival of the great Duke from the Congress at Vienna, to take command of the assembling army, which was indeed a motley one, being composed of British, Dutch, Belgians, Hanoverians, Brunswickers, etc. Many of our own were weak second battalions, chiefly those who had been under Sir Thomas Graham; and the foreigners were mostly young levies, the Brunswickers and Hanoverians being for the greater part mere boys. Many of the Dutch and Belgians had served under Napoleon's eagles, and had, of course, strong French proclivities.

The headquarters of our cavalry was at Ninove, fifteen miles from Brussels, and I saw some 7000 reviewed before old Blücher. Both men and horses appeared very creditable, and the day was very fine. I was

---

1. Shave, *i.e.*, a false rumour.

present on the occasion, and also when the Duke reviewed the Brunswick troops, some 9000 strong, at Vilvoorde, six miles from Brussels, on the Antwerp road. They were well clothed and accoutred, and the Duke of Brunswick seemed proud to exhibit them.

I shall now vary my tale by introducing a bit of gossip. I was sitting one afternoon in the park with an elderly Belgian lady, when a very great man walked past us, and immediately after a carriage drew up at an entrance on the opposite side of the park, and a lady alighted, who was joined by the great man. My friend and I, prompted by curiosity, arose to see the result of the junction, following with our eyes the lady and gentleman until they descended into a hollow, where the trees completely screened them. We then perceived another carriage arrive, from which an old lady descended, whom I recognised as Lady M. N., who went peering about as if looking for someone or something, but was completely baffled by the tactics of the lady and gentleman, and left the park *re infectâ*. She was clearly in search of her daughter, Lady F. W., of whom "busy fame whispered light things." But I must proceed to matters of more moment.

CHAPTER 3

Ligny

Early on the 15th June 1815, we learned that the French were crossing the frontier at Charleroi. In the evening, about seven o'clock, I got a summons to the Quartermaster-General's office, Sir William Delancey,[1] our chief, having received the Duke's orders for collecting the allied army.

For two or three hours I was engaged with others in writing out orders for the several divisions to march, which were expedited by means of hussars, men selected for their steadiness. Each was told the rate at which he was to proceed, and time for reaching his destination. It was his duty to bring back the cover of the despatch, on which the officer receiving it had to state the exact time of its delivery. I thought my duty for the day was ended when the despatches had been sent off; but my friend, Colonel Torrens, whispered in my ear that he had put me in for a ride, and Sir W. Delancey handed me a packet, saying. "I am told you know the road to Ninove; here is a letter for Colonel Cathcart; be as speedy as possible."

In a few minutes I was in the saddle, wending my way in the darkness to Ninove, by a cross road. As I approached that place, I found lights in adjacent villages and men stirring about, indicating that the order for marching had been issued. Colonel Cathcart was the assistant quartermaster-general to the whole of the cavalry, and an excellent officer, to whom I was well known. "You may tell Delancey that in an hour or so we shall be on our march to Nivelles, in accordance

---

1. Sir William Howe De Lancy, whose sister married Sir Hudson Lowe, succeeded the latter as quarter master- general in the Low Countries early in June 1815, and was killed at Waterloo. Of him the Duke of Wellington wrote in his Waterloo despatch: "This officer is a serious loss to His Majesty's service, and to me at this moment."

with the order received."

On my way back. I fell in with several officers of rank, making for their troops, having hurried from the Duchess of Richmond's ball; and I, knowing all the arrangements for the army generally, was able to tell them what roads to take in order to intercept their divisions. I could boast of a good acquaintance with the greater part of Belgium; for, besides having been often sent about to arrange for quartering troops, I had been employed by our active chief, Sir Hudson Lowe, in examining and reporting upon various routes between Brussels and the French frontier; indeed, when any distant business required the presence of an officer of the department, it commonly fell to me, probably as a junior.

My return to Brussels from Ninove was at a leisurely pace, and it may have been about four o'clock on the morning of the 16th that I, threading the Rue de la Madeleine, reached the beautiful Place Royale, and heard sounds of movement in the park adjacent. On entering it, I found a large body of our troops in line, which their commander, the redoubtable Picton, was inspecting, accompanied by his staff. I reined in my horse, and awaited the termination of the ceremony. It was truly a splendid division, of which Picton might feel proud. The order was given for the whole to form subdivisions, and then "quick march." I posted myself at the Hotel Bellevue to see them pass. First came a battalion of the 95th Rifles (now the Rifle Brigade), dressed in dark green, and with black accoutrements. The 28th Regiment followed, then the 42nd Highlanders, marching so steadily that the sable plumes of their bonnets scarcely vibrated. The 79th and 92nd, both Highlanders, were also there. The full kilted dress may have somewhat of a theatrical aspect, but is certainly very imposing—indeed, an ordinary battalion of our infantry has a mean appearance when contrasted with the wearers of the "garb of old Gaul." I thus saw something of "the pomp and circumstance of glorious war," and heard the last of the measured tread of the troops, which alone disturbed the stillness of the morning. Forth they went by the Porte de Namur :—

> And Ardennes waves above them her green leaves,
> Dewy with Nature's teardrops, as they pass,
> Grieving, if aught inanimate e'er grieves,
> Over the unreturning brave,—alas!
> Ere evening to be trodden like the grass
> Which now beneath them, but above shall grow
> In its next verdure, when this fiery mass

Of living valour, rolling on the foe
And burning with high hope, shall moulder cold and low.

These lines truly tell the fate of many hundreds of those noble soldiers, who marched forth confident of victory; for ere the sun, whose early rays gilded their bright arms, had set, grim death had made sad havoc among them. But not in vain was the sacrifice, since it must be admitted that Picton's indomitable energy, and the determined pluck of his regiments, saved the important position of Quatre Bras, repelling every effort of Ney and his *corps d'armée*, until other troops arrived from Nivelles, and helped to secure that point; and they did this after performing a forced march of twenty miles, oppressed by summer heat, and the heavy weight of knapsack, arms, and ammunition.

I think it was about 2 p.m. of that day when Brussels first heard the booming of distant guns; and then began the cry of *Sauve qui peut* among the numerous English families residing there. All the post horses were soon engaged in transporting them to Antwerp or to Ghent; but numbers were forced to remain, at least for the present. As to the inhabitants, they had seen so much of armies traversing their city in the preceding year, that the aspect of things seemed little more in their eyes than the threatening of a whirlwind, which might or might not seriously and injuriously affect them. Besides, half of the inhabitants were French at heart, and if Napoleon should prevail, they would only be welcoming friends.

The cannonade soon became almost continuous, seeming very near; and as I knew that the Duke and headquarters staff had gone in the direction of Waterloo, I felt it to be only my proper course to endeavour to join headquarters; the roar of the cannon, moreover, aroused my boyish ardour, and I was speedily mounted and on my way. I had not got over many miles, when I overtook Colonel Nicolay,[2] of my own corps, and, of course, pulled up to join him. As he did not suggest my pushing on, I felt bound to remain with him, and accommodate myself to his sober pace; so we jogged on together at a far more gentle rate than that at which I had been riding.

While traversing the forest of Soignies, the cannonade was so loud as to lead us to believe that the battle was raging within very few miles of us, probably near Waterloo. On emerging, however, from its glades, the firing seemed to be more distant than we had supposed. Just as we reached the farm of La Haye Sainte, so celebrated as a post of impor-

---

2. In after years Governor of Mauritius, an excellent officer and wise administrator.

tance in the great battle of the 18th, we met Sir George Scovell, one of the Duke's trusted staff officers. He told us that our troops had been successful in holding their position at Quatre Bras, against heavy odds, up to the moment of his coming away, but that the firing had seemed to follow him. This was bad, the inference being that our troops were retiring, and, coupled with the condition of Sir George's horse, which was white with foam, indicative of extreme haste, caused us sinister augury.

Pressing on, we reached the long village of Genappe, and began to meet wounded men and stragglers, to some of whom we spoke and gleaned hope that the Duke was still maintaining himself at Quatre Bras. The cannonade appeared now to come from the left of our road, for which at the time we could not account; but doubtless the heavy firing we had been hearing proceeded from the great battle of Ligny, and not from the action at Quatre Bras, the direction of the wind accounting for this mistake.

After leaving Genappe we encountered quite a stream of disabled soldiers, British and foreign. As two Brunswickers passed, I heard one of them say, "*Unser Herzog ist lodt*" ("Our Duke is dead"), which, alas! proved but too true.

He rushed into the field, and, foremost fighting, fell.

Dressed in black, having their *shakos* ornamented (if so the term may be used) with a skull and cross bones, the Brunswick soldiers wore a grim aspect. I was told that the dress and bones were to be worn as a perpetual mourning for the Duke who fell at the Battle of Jena, in 1806, father of the hero who was killed at Quatre Bras.

The Brunswick contingent had been for some weeks stationed at Vilvoorde, five miles from Brussels, as I have mentioned, and I frequently saw the Duke on occasions of ceremony, and admired his soldier-like appearance and gallant bearing.

On nearing Quatre Bras we fell in with a remarkable group of human beings, clustered upon some sort of wheel carriage, that turned out to be a Dutch 12-pounder gun, upon which sat or clung a dozen or more of wounded men, bloody and dirty, with head or limb bound up, and among them two or three females. It was with great surprise that I heard my name issue from the cluster, and, on close inspection, perceived that it proceeded from Brough, of the 44th, whom I had last seen at Bergen-op-Zoom. He said that Picton's division had suffered very severely, but kept its ground; that he was himself wounded, and but too happy to avail himself of his present seat on the gun-carriage, feeling, however, as if the joking would kill him outright, and exclaiming, "Oh! that I had my horse." How his countenance gleamed when I told him that we had just passed his handsome Andalusian, an animal he had brought from Spain, and of which he was exceedingly proud.

CHAPTER 4

Quatre Bras

The shades of evening were creeping over the scene of action at Quatre Bras when we arrived there, and too late to see Ney's last effort against the position; but considerable bodies of the enemy seemed still to wear a threatening" aspect, but, save by a few shots of artillery and the popping of skirmishers, there was no more firing that evening. The Duke remained for some time longer near the Bois de Bossu, intently watching the dark masses in our front, which stood scarcely beyond the range of our most advanced field-pieces; but it was evident the business of the day was over. Some of our acquaintances belonging to the staff gave us, in the meantime, an account of the severe and bloody battle; all agreeing that our troops had never been more severely pressed in maintaining their position; it was also said that the Duke had exposed his person more than on any former occasion, and that his escaping without a wound was wonderful. Then followed an eulogium of *our* troops; and the old Brunswick regiment of cavalry— so long in our service—was well spoken of; but the foreign troops generally had been disappointing.[1]

The next question was that of quarters for the night—not for the troops who had so hardly fought; they had the cold ground for their bed, with the canopy of heaven for a cover-lid, and short commons, if any, for supper—but for the staff, who could go where they pleased, and get housed. Genappe was scarcely a couple of miles in the rear, and would, we know, be headquarters; so thither Colonel Nicolay and I went, with other staff officers. On entering the principal *auberge*, we

---

1. This is scarcely fair. The stand made by Prince Bernhard of Saxe-Weimar at the beginning of the fight at Quatre Bras was most creditable, and but far him and Perponcher's decision to hold that place—quite independent of Wellington who was far in the rear—it would have been lost. See Rose's *Napoleon*, 2. 462.

22

found a long table, with covers laid for at least twenty persons, the arrangement of which an officer of the Duke's staff was superintending, acting as a sort of *major domo*; there were hampers of wine in the room, from which he was selecting bottles for the table. On observing my companion, whose rank entitled him to some consideration, he proposed his remaining to sup with His Grace; the invitation was, however, declined, so we left the House and succeeded in getting a billet from the mayor on a worthy shoemaker, who received us very hospitably, desiring his wife to boil a chicken and fry an *omelette*.

After despatching these with much gusto, we retired to excellent beds. It was then after eleven, and I had just fallen asleep, when a tremendous clatter of horses in the street caused me to jump out of bed in some surprise; when I found that the horsemen were moving in the direction of our army. I tried to recompose myself to sleep, but the incessant clatter of hoofs, jingling of steel scabbards, and rattle of artillery kept me awake for hours, as I thought. This was the whole, or nearly so, of the British cavalry, which had moved from Ninove by Nivelles, and were proceeding towards Quatre Bras.

The last horseman of the rear-guard had scarcely passed, when I judged it was time for me to be up and to horse. Before daylight, I was again with the army, and when the sun rose, a truly magnificent spectacle presented itself, as I rode along that part of the Nivelles and Namur *chaussée*, behind which most of our divisions were ranged in position. There was no point from which the eye could command the whole of the ground occupied, none being sufficiently elevated; and besides, the Bois de Bossu, a wood of some extent, closed the prospect on the right; the tall rye, moreover, which mostly covered the undulating land, served to conceal most of the infantry, breaking, as it were, the continuity of line. Still, the extent of ground it covered, the large number of guns visible, with lighted match, ready to open their destructive fire, and the heavy bodies of cavalry in rear, gave evidence that a powerful army now awaited the onset of the enemy.

In our front, and perhaps a couple of miles distant, the prevailing verdure of the fields was broken here and there by dark patches, known to be the masses of the French; but they must have had some troops nearer to us, but hidden by undulations of the ground, as a support to skirmishers, who kept up a constant popping, responded to by those of our own, in the low ground between the armies, where grew some straggling willows and stunted alders, which, together with the partially standing crops, afforded sufficient cover to render the firing a useless waste of ammunition.

A few changes were made in the disposition of the troops after the Duke of Wellington arrived on the ground, soon after daylight; arms were then piled, and the men, still wearied with their exertions of fighting and marching the day before, lay down to get a little rest. The Duke too, after riding about, and satisfying himself that all things were in order, dismounted and sat down on the ground very near the point of intersection of the *chaussées*, called "les Quatre Bras." He was habited in his usual field costume, namely. a short blue frock coat, and shorter cloak of the same colour, leather pantaloons, and Hessian boots; his plain and low cocked-hat was surmounted by no feather, such as we see in the statue near Apsley House: the large drooping plume we borrowed from the Prussians, and it became pretty general amongst our staff officers after we got to Paris.

On the Duke's black English cockade were attached three very small ones, of about an inch in diameter, being those of Spain, Portugal, and the Netherlands, in token of his holding rank in the armies of those countries. I remained for some time at a short distance from the great man, who occasionally addressed a word to Lord Fitzroy Somerset, Barnes, Delancey, and others of his principal staff officers. He was then awaiting the return of Sir Alexander Gordon, an *aide-de-camp*, who had been sent off between six and seven o'clock, escorted by a squadron of the 10th Hussars, to learn something of the Prussians, of whose defeat at Ligny, we, that is the army at large, were in ignorance, though the Duke and his chief officers had been apprised of it the night before.[2]

I availed myself of this period of quietude to go and examine all the ground which had been so hardly contested the day before. Descending by the Charleroi road, I looked around some farmhouses, not far from the point of Quatre Bras, in and about which were many wounded men; and I noticed numerous shot holes in their roofs and walls.

It was for possession of these that severe struggles had been made, the gallant French *cuirassiers* having repeatedly charged past the houses, even up to "les Quatre Bras;" hence, not only was the corn entirely

---

2. This was not so. The Prussians most unaccountably did not apprise Wellington of their retreat. It was not until Gordon's patrol found out the truth—on which was based the order to Picton to retire on Waterloo, mentioned below—that a Prussian orderly came to the Duke's headquarters and confirmed the news. See Rose's *Napoleon*, 2 479.

trodden down for a considerable distance on each side of the road, but it was cut up, and trampled, just as may be seen in a London street on an occasion of sickness. The ground was strewed with battered helmets, damaged cuirasses, broken swords and muskets, shattered gun-carriages, and other signs of fierce strife; and that it had been a bloody contest was shown by the manly form of many a bold *cuirassier*, lying stretched by the side of a dead opponent.

An eyewitness told me that on one occasion eight or ten bold fellows had ridden into a farmyard, in order to clear it of some of our men, and, endeavouring to get out on the opposite side, were, to a man, mown down by a couple of our guns, like pigeons from a trap. I then rode towards the advanced posts in front of our left, passing over the ground where the 42nd Highlanders had been surprised by the *cuirassiers*, who, concealed by the tall rye, were upon them before they could even think of forming square. Here lay many of the "unreturning brave," whom I had seen leave Brussels full of "high hope" but a few short hours before. The corn there was only partially trodden down, and hence, although the dead and wounded were many, the eye detected but few at a time.

The dead lay in every attitude, but generally on their backs, with placid countenances, evincing little trace of suffering in their last moments, I occasionally spoke to and endeavoured to cheer some of the wounded. Not a murmur did any of the poor fellows utter; they knew they would be aired for when circumstances should permit, and meanwhile bore hunger, thirst, and pain with manly resignation. It is not in battle only that the British soldier evinces his fortitude and thorough manliness; his high qualities are equally apparent when he lies on the bed of suffering. Let us rejoice that the legislature and country at large have at length been awakened to the soldier's merits, and to his unworthy treatment in times past, and that there is some promise of amendment for the future.

Keeping a sharp lookout lest any French horsemen should pounce upon me amongst the tall rye, I rode along the irregular line of our skirmishers; but indeed there was little risk, all firing having ceased. Having satisfied my curiosity, I was returning towards the headquarters staff, when my attention was drawn to a group near the Bois de Bossu, and, on moving towards them, I recognised the uniform of the 33rd Regiment, of which I knew a few of the officers, and witnessed a most affecting and impressive scene. On the ground lay a tall form, enveloped in a military cloak, around which were standing, bareheaded, three or four officers; two soldiers were leaning on their spades, wherewith a shallow grave had been dug. One of the officers was endeavouring, in broken accents, to read our beautiful burial service; another, Ralph Gore, stood motionless as a statue, with eye fixed on the cloaked mass at his feet; young Haigh, a boy of eighteen, was crying like a child; even the hardy soldiers seemed powerfully affected.

I needed not to be told whose body lay there. Throwing myself from my horse, I too became a mourner. When the service ceased, I cast an inquiring look towards Haigh, who, stooping down, withdrew from the corpse a portion of its covering, and, as I expected, exposed to my gaze the remarkably handsome features of Arthur Gore. Poor fellow! but two short weeks before, when employed on some mission, having to pass the village in which the 33rd were quartered, I fell in with young Gore, who prevailed upon me to remain and meet at dinner his elder brother and Haigh. We had all been at the Military College together, and left it about the same time.

As may be supposed, we passed a right merry evening, and little did I then think where and under what sad circumstances we were again to meet. Poor Haigh was killed on the following day at Waterloo, His name, with that of Arthur Gore, and several other fine young fellows of their regiment, is recorded on a tablet in the little church at Waterloo.

It was remarked by the good people of Brussels, how very youthful were our officers generally. Accustomed to the burly forms and bushy whiskers of the French officers, it surprised them to see lieutenants, and even captains, still in their teens. Contrasting the quiet and gentlemanly deportment of these with the more *brusque* manners of the French and German officers, which they had been taught to think more militarily, being moreover in great ignorance of the exploits of our Peninsular army, I became aware that we were little thought of as soldiers, and the vast superiority of our navy was more than hinted. The great battle at their gates must have dispelled their delusion, and, no doubt, if circumstances should ever again take British troops into their country, our lads will neither be twitted with their youth nor the superiority of our "blue-jackets."

The conqueror of Scinde is reported to have said that he never wished to see a captain above six-and-twenty; I must not stop now to discuss the question. whether young or old officers are best in the junior grades, but will hazard an opinion that, for battle, the headlong dash of the English lad of twenty is better than the calculating coolness of riper years. And even as regards soldiers, I may cite the opinion of an experienced officer who served throughout the Peninsular campaigns, and that of Waterloo—Fullarton, of the Rifles: he said, "Give me young soldiers, old ones are apt to become too cunning."

On returning to the place where I had left the Duke, when I went on my ramble round the outposts, I found him still seated on the ground, where he remained till Gordon and his escort returned with jaded horses, soon after ten o'clock. On hearing his report, the Duke said a few words to Delancey, who, observing me at hand, directed me to find Sir Thomas Picton, and tell him to make immediate preparation for withdrawing to Waterloo. I found Picton at a farmhouse a short distance along the Charleroi *chaussée*, who gave me a surly acknowledgment of the order; he evidently disliked to retire from a position he had so gallantly held the day before, and no wonder!

The first intimation that the army was about to retire was the getting in the wounded; troopers were sent to the front, who placed such disabled men as could manage to sit, on their horses, they themselves rendering support on foot. At times a poor fellow might be seen toppling from side to side, requiring two men to keep him on his seat: the horses moving gently, as if conscious that their motions were torturing their suffering riders. Some again required to be carried in a blanket, so that every man found with life in him was in one way or another brought in and sent to the rear. It was about midday ere this important duty was completed, and the troops then began to move off by brigades, in such a manner as should prevent the enemy from observing what we were about.

I was immediately told to ride off to Mont St Jean, where I was to meet the quartermaster-general. I accordingly made for Genappe, and, as the road was filled with troops, and I cared nothing for the poor farmer's interests, took my way across his cornfields, gaining the village by a short cut. There I found sad confusion prevailing, country waggons with stores, ammunition tumbrils, provision waggons, and wounded men, so blocking the village street that it was scarcely possible for anyone to pass along it. Aware of the great importance of freeing the defile, at a moment when our retreating troops might be pressed by the foe, I instantly set to work to try and remedy the disorder.

Let the reader picture to himself a single police constable at the point where Gracechurch Street crosses Cornhill, at a moment when, as far as he can see, all the passages are choked by omnibuses, drays,

waggons, carts, cabs, carriages, and other *impedimenta*, while that bewildered functionary is vainly endeavouring to restore order, and he
will have some idea of the difficulty I experienced in executing my
self-imposed task. Happily I knew a few pithy objurgations in two or
three languages, very familiar to the ears of those I had to deal with;
and these, together with the free application of the flat of my sword
to the backs of the most refractory, proved efficacious. Whilst engaged
in this scene of confusion, I felt some one clap me on the shoulder,
and found it to be Sir W. Delancey, who said, "You are well employed
here, remain and keep the way clear; I shall not want you at Mont St
Jean,"

CHAPTER 5

Mont St. Jean

My duty as a military constable over, I pushed for Brussels *viâ*
Mont St Jean and Waterloo, not sorry to escape further duty that day,
as well as anxious to see about my servants, horses, and baggage, having left no orders with my men on the previous day. That night the
rain fell in torrents, drenching our troops to the skin, who, arriving
late at their position, had no time to prepare even the most trifling
protection against the storm.

I have stated that much bustle prevailed at Brussels on the 16th
June, during the fighting at Quatre Bras and Ligny, but It was trifling as compared with the disorder I witnessed on the morning of
the 18th, when the Park, Place Royale, and streets adjacent, were not
only encumbered by vehicles of all kinds, but also by multitudes of
wounded men, who had flocked in during the night from the Prussian
and British armies. The city being defenceless, no hospitals had been
prepared for them, nor, owing to the suddenness of the sanguinary
battles, had any steps been taken by the Municipality to provide even
temporary shelter; hence the poor fellows were compelled to remain
in the streets until the authorities could devise measures for their relief, or that, compassionating their forlorn situation, charitable citizens
took them in and administered to their necessities.

It is pleasing to record how much Christian charity was shown by
many at that distressing time, a single family having, as I was credibly
informed afterwards, received and tended no less than fifty wounded
Englishmen, a gratifying tribute of respect for the character of our
soldiery, who indeed had earned golden opinions among the worthy
Bruxellois during the long period of their sojourn in the city. The
residence of that family of good Samaritans was in the Place de Lou-
vain, but I regret to say I have forgotten their name.

Besides the thousands of wounded, there were present numbers of marauders, chiefly cowardly rascals who had abandoned their colours, and were prowling about for plunder; these were mostly the scum of Blücher's army—not true Prussians, I trust, though clad in Prussian uniforms; they stole several horses left by British officers who were in the field, besides committing other depredations. My excellent friend Colonel Torrens, afterwards adjutant-general in Bengal, was robbed of two fine animals, for which he had paid a large sum only a few days before. On the night of the 17th, he had been sent by the Duke to direct Sir Charles Colville to fall back from Braine le Comte to Hal; and after performing this duty, had ridden on to Brussels for a fresh horse, when, to his dismay, the two in question were gone from his stable. Knowing that I intended to pass the previous night in the city, he was proceeding to my quarters, that I might assist in trying to recover the animals. I met him on the morning of the 18th as I was about to start for the army; we wasted some hours in a fruitless search, but the horses were seen no more.

In order to show that we did not suspect the Prussians without reason of perpetrating this and other robberies of horses, I shall here relate an incident that afterwards occurred in France. I was sent back on duty from Pont St Maxence to some distance in the rear, when, falling in with a squadron of Prussians, I remarked a trooper in the ranks leading two English horses, which I looked at narrowly, hoping to recognise those stolen from my friend Torrens. A little further on, and while the squadron was still in sight, I met one of our commissaries, who hurriedly asked if I had noticed any English horses with it; on my answering in the affirmative, he hastened on, while I, rather curious to see the end of the affair, rode after him.

No sooner did he see the horses than he seized the bridle of one of them, which action being resisted by the dragoon, the commissary drew his sword and flourished it over the fellow's head; meanwhile, the officer at the head of the squadron, perceiving that something was wrong, and the Englishman being no linguist, I explained that the gentleman with a long feather and gold epaulettes, who in the eye of the Prussians was a full colonel at least, claimed the horses as his property. Upon which he said a few words to the soldier, who at once surrendered them. Surely both honesty and discipline must have been at a low ebb in that squadron, when a private could thus be marching in the ranks, leading a couple of stolen horses. The commissary told me that his stable having been broken open the night before, and as

Prussians were near, he had rightly suspected them of the theft. But to return from this digression.

After relinquishing our bootless search, Colonel Torrens and I started for Waterloo. The clouds were heavy that morning, but the pouring rain of the night was followed by a gentle drizzle, which continued to fall long after the battle began. We were scarcely beyond the Namur Gate when we heard firing, but not heavy, and apparently more distant than the position near Waterloo; it, however, caused us to push on through the forest as fast as the state of the road would permit. The quantity of rain which had fallen had made it fetlock deep in mud on either side of the pavement, where we were forced to ride, the paved portion of the road being entirely occupied by wheel carriages of various kinds, hastening to the rear; indeed, the whole of the wide road was at times so encumbered, as to oblige us to leave it altogether, and thread our way among the trees. The immediate rear of every great army, when actually engaged, will always present scenes of confusion; but on that occasion the suddenness and rapidity of our operations, the diversity of troops forming the Anglo-allied force, together with the necessity for everything to move upon a single road, created an extraordinary amount of disorder.

The road from Brussels to Waterloo enters the forest of Soignies at about two miles from the city, and is sheltered by noble trees nearly as far as the hamlet of Mont St Jean, which lies more than a mile beyond the village of Waterloo; the breadth of the forest in that part is some seven or eight miles. Ere we had got half way through it, the roar of cannon became loud and prolonged; but we needed not this testimony to prove that the battle was raging, for we encountered numbers of affrighted fugitives, nearly all wearing foreign uniforms, from some of whom we learned, as they hurried breathless along, that our army had given way, and all was lost. This was startling news, and at first we knew not what to make of it; still, we could not believe that things were so bad as that, and concluded that probably some of the foreign troops might have been routed, but hoped that the British remained staunch.

All apprehension was, however, banished by meeting a wounded staff officer, whom we knew, who informed us that when he left the field the army held its position, and had just repelled a severe attack on its right. On clearing the forest, we came in sight of the position, and saw that all was right. I have no intention of eking out these personal recollections by giving any account of the general features of the battle; the changes have been too often rung upon them for my poor pen to dilate on the repeated efforts of the enemy to dislodge us from our ground, which was maintained throughout the day against fearful odds by the determined pluck of our chief, and, I may say with truth, the courage and determination of the British troops. This reminds me of a trifling incident that occurred a few weeks before. The Duke was inspecting one of his divisions, when his quartermaster-general, not Delancey, said something of the fine and soldier-like appearance of the men, "Yes," observed His Grace," but wait till you see those fellows fight." This was repeated to me by the quartermaster-general.

I would here remark that whatever may be the defects discernible in these pages, they will state nothing but what I either actually witnessed myself, or what I know really to have occurred. Possibly many of my recollections may be deemed of little interest; but as an eminent person observed to me recently, *à propos* of an incident represented in Sir William Allan's fine illustration of the battle, "Waterloo has lost none of its interest;" a remark, by the way, which engendered in me the idea of scribbling these pages, As the last gleaner lingering over a field that has been searched over and over, but few ears of corn could be expected to fall to my share, and so, not to leave my field quite empty-handed, I am compelled to pick up a few straws of little value, which, coming from such a field as Waterloo, are perhaps worth preserving.

As few can have any idea of the number of persons usually attached to the headquarters of a large army, it may be as well to state that the Duke's tail at Waterloo comprised at least forty officers. There was his personal staff, consisting of his military secretary and six or eight *aides-de-camp*, the adjutant and quartermaster-generals, each with a suite of half-a-dozen officers; the commanding officers of engineers and artillery with their following. Besides our own people, we had Generals Alava, Müffling, and Vincent, attended by their *aides-de-camp*, so that we formed an imposing cavalcade, sadly diminished at the close of the battle, as will be seen.

It will readily be conceived, that none save individuals attached to the headquarters staff can possibly move about so as to see what takes place in various parts of the field of battle, all others being necessarily confined within a more or less limited sphere of action and of vision, and therefore only cognizant of events occurring in their immediate vicinity. Hence a person may see much fighting and yet know very little about the battle in which he is taking part. Probably there never

32

was a battle when a General-in-Chief afforded to the headquarters staff better opportunities of witnessing its principal events than at Waterloo; for wherever there was an attack, thither went the Duke, exposing himself to the hottest fire, as if, like Father Murphy in the Irish Rebellion, he could catch and pocket the enemy's bullets; indeed, his escaping without a wound was marvellous.

On one occasion especially I trembled for his safety; it was during an attack on the left of La Haye Sainte, between three and four o'clock, when he remained for many minutes exposed to a heavy fire of musketry. All the staff, except a single *aide-de-camp*, had received a signal to keep back, in order not to attract the enemy's fire; we remained, therefore, under the brow of the elevated ground, and, the better to keep out of observation, dismounted. As I looked over my saddle, I could just trace the outlines of the Duke and his horse amidst the smoke, standing very near the Highlanders of Picton's division, bearing a resemblance to the statue in Hyde Park when partially shrouded by fog, while the balls—and they came thickly—hissed harmlessly over our heads. It was a time of intense anxiety, for had the Duke fallen, heaven only knows what might have been the result of the fight! I have said that a single *aide-de-camp* was in attendance on that perilous occasion, Lord Arthur Hill, the most portly young man in the army, who, when a lad at the Military College, was always called "Fat Hill;" being at a little distance behind the Duke, I can only suppose that he escaped being riddled, by not finding himself directly within the line of fire.

At times the situation of the staff, like that of the troops, when standing to be pounded by round and grape shot, was trying enough, while at others it was very exciting; but nothing that occurred seemed to produce any effect on the Duke, whom I had frequent opportunities of observing, as he would often turn and counter-march, thereby closely passing all who followed. His countenance and demeanour were at all times quite calm, rarely speaking to any one, save to give an order, or send a message; indeed, he generally rode quite alone, that is, no one was at his side, seeming unconscious even of the presence of his own troops, whilst his eye kept scanning intently those of his great opponent. Occasionally he would stop and peer for a few seconds through the large field telescope which he carried in his right hand; and this his horse, the docile Copenhagen, his old Peninsular favourite, permitted without a sign of impatience.

Thus he would promenade in front of the troops, along the crest of their position, watching the enemy's preparations for their attacks.

I well remember that once, when he was about to pass in front of a battalion of Nassau troops, two *aides-de-camp* rushed forward and said, "My Lord Duke, they are Nassauers." At first I thought he was going to persist in going on, and felt heartily glad when he turned his horse and went in another direction. These Nassauers formed part of the Dutch or Belgian contingent, and had served under the French eagles; indeed, their arms, dress, and general bearing were perfectly French; it looked a splendid battalion, but inspired us with no confidence. Unquestionably it was only prudent of the Duke to avoid passing in their front, for the drawing of a single trigger, at such a moment, might have done a thousand times more injury to the cause of Europe than was effected by all Napoleon's cannon.

It is but just to state that the battalion in question was the only one, of a body of three thousand men, that remained on its ground in the first line; all the rest had clearly "no stomach for the fight," as they coolly withdrew early in the day out of harm's way. I should mention, however, that they were not the only soldiers who preferred to be in the rear, as great numbers of the foreign troops generally were of the same way of thinking; but we must bear in mind that there was a powerful feeling in favour of Napoleon, especially among the Dutch and Belgians, thousands of those then brought against him having long fought under his eagles. Then, as regards the Hanoverians and Brunswickers, they were mostly very young soldiers, who had not been embodied many months, likely to make good ones in time; but Waterloo was a trying battle for veterans, and bodies of mere recruits could not be expected to withstand such troops as were brought against them. The wonder is that they stood at all.

It certainly showed a vast amount of nerve in the Duke to hazard a battle against Napoleon with so motley a force as his army presented; but, under the circumstances, he could not do otherwise. He has written it as his opinion, that "Forty thousand British troops formed a good position anywhere." He had not more than thirty thousand at Waterloo,[1] but they sufficed to form a good position. "I never saw our infantry behave so well," he wrote soon afterwards. Well might he say, as I have quoted already, "You should see those fellows fight"

Happily "those fellows "fought under the *prestige* of many Peninsula battles, in which, as they had been chiefly defensive on our part,

---

1. The British troops at Waterloo numbered 33,990. Perhaps, however, the King's German Legion (5800) is here included, which makes the number up to nearly 30,000.

they had learned how to repel the fierce onslaughts of their gallant opponents, and the same tactics carried them triumphantly on this grand occasion. The coolness with which the "thin red line" awaited the approach of massive close columns, pouring in a deadly fire at the right moment, [was splendid], then [came] a rushing charge with a British cheer, and the business was done, or, in the Duke's language, "the enemy just came on in the old style, and were driven off in the old style."

Having alluded to the wholesale abandonment of the field by some of our auxiliaries, let me mention here, that, having been sent to order up a battery of Dutch guns, which stood in reserve close to the farm of Mont St Jean, a staff officer whom I met told me that just inside the forest were swarms of foreign soldiers. After delivering my message to the commander of the guns, who refused to move them, alleging that he had expended all his ammunition, I peeped into the skirts of the forest, and truly felt astonished; entire companies seemed there, with regularly piled arms, fires blazing under cooking kettles, while the men lay about smoking as coolly as if no enemy were within a day's march! That such a scene should have presented itself so close to the battle then raging, is, I believe, wholly unprecedented. General Müffling, in his account of Waterloo, estimates the runaways hidden in the forest at 10,000—a number not, I believe, exaggerated.[2]

---

2. See Professor Oman's article in the *Nineteenth Century* for October 1900 on the bad behaviour of the Dutch-Belgians at Waterloo.

CHAPTER 6

The Advance

The admirable discipline of our troops, including the German Legion, which did such good service in the Peninsula, was conspicuous throughout the day; more especially when the French formidable looking *cuirassiers* were riding between and round the squares, contemplating the bristling bayonets, which they dared not approach; while not a shot was fired at them, as any firing might have caused some degree of unsteadiness. This extraordinary state of things may have prevailed for more than half-an-hour: a useless bravado, for, after the failure of serious charges previously made against our squares of steel, it was unlikely that loose demonstrations were calculated to disturb them. And, indeed, as to the so-called charges, I do not think that on a single occasion actual collision occurred. I many times saw the gallant and daring *cuirassiers* come on with boldness to within some twenty or thirty yards of a square, when, seeing the steady firmness of our men, they invariably edged away and retired.

Sometimes they would halt and gaze at the triple row of bayonets, when two or three brave officers would advance and strive by voice and gesture to urge the attack, raising their helmets aloft on their sabres, the better to be seen by their irresolute men; but all in vain, as no efforts could make them close with the terrible bayonets, and meet certain destruction. Had their efforts been directed against squares of the second line, they would have had some chance of success; as I repeatedly noticed unsteadiness among our foreigners, men running from them to the rear, when two or three staff officers would intercept them and drive them back. I more than once assisted in this, and was surprised at the ease with which the fellows were driven back to their duty. Respecting cavalry attacks against good infantry formed in squares, it is admitted by, I may say, all officers of any experience, that

36

until cannon has taken effect, so as to produce disorder in a square, they are worse than useless, tending to give confidence on one side, while they dishearten the other.

Now and then we of the staff had to run, in order to get away from the enemy's cavalry, but, being well mounted, were soon out of their reach; but on one occasion my friend Torrens was caused much annoyance; his horse, a hard-mouthed animal, actually ran away with him, so that when he returned he was received with a little bantering, and complimented on the speed of his horse. Another, a very young fellow, was soon after carried at full speed to the rear, a freak for which his rider could not at the moment account. It happened thus. The French cavalry having made a rush upon a battery commanded by Major Lloyd, he, with his officers and gunners, sought refuge in a square of the Guards; Lloyd, however, did not enter the square, but found shelter under its lee. When the enemy withdrew, the six guns remained untouched; seeing which, Lloyd ran up to them, followed by the young staff officer in question, and, seizing a rammer, tried one of the pieces, which he found loaded; this he fired upon the retiring foe, then not a hundred and fifty yards distant; a second gun was also found loaded, and the *cuirassiers* treated with another parting salute. This was the work of only a minute or two, and as yet the gunners had not returned.

The officer above alluded to was in the act of looking into an ammunition box for the means of charging another gun, when his horse suddenly wheeled round, plunged violently, and went off at a racing pace to the rear (happily), the rider losing his cocked-hat at the same moment. On mastering his steed, and returning to the front, a greeting, with some allusion to John Gilpin, met his ear. Having recovered his hat, and rejoined those to whom he had afforded amusement, the *aide-de-camp* of General Alava told him his horse was wounded, and bleeding very much. On examination, it was found that a ball had entered the animal's belly, which fully accounted for his erratic freak. The brave Lloyd fell soon afterwards while directing his guns.

I have already said that in action few can know much of what is going on at a distance from their immediate sphere of observation. I shall here give an instance. About two o'clock an attack in great force was made upon Picton's division on our left. On the enemy being driven off in confusion, our cavalry charged down upon them, killing and wounding a great number, and capturing upwards of two thousand, who were at once sent under an escort of Dutch soldiers to

Brussels. An hour or more afterwards, happening to be on the right of our line, I came upon a battalion of the Rifles, many of whose officers I knew. The men were lying down at the moment, and Captain Full-arton, with the officers of his company, came round me to ask what I knew of the action at other points of the field. I then told them of the attack on Picton, the repulse of the French, and their loss, especially in prisoners, of all which they knew nothing whatever. Many years afterwards, I met Fullarton at Halifax, Nova Scotia, when he reminded me of our meeting at Waterloo, and how I had gladdened the battalion to which he belonged by the intelligence I then communicated. It was posted on the right of the Nivelles road, not far from Hougomont, and, I think, had not then been called upon to act, but was awaiting the progress of the battle with nervous anxiety. Fullarton was a brave and good officer, and had seen much fighting under Wellington in the Peninsula; he died when Commandant at Halifax, and I saw him laid in his grave.

After my fruitless mission to the Dutch battery above alluded to, at the farm of Mont St Jean, I was returning to the front, when I fell in with Colonel Nicolay, and we were proceeding together along the *chaussée* towards La Haye Sainte, when two or three cannon balls came bounding along it; they were nearly spent, as it is termed, though retaining force enough to kill either man or horse. When I proposed that we should quit the *chaussée* and get out of the line of fire, the colonel scorned to give way to a few cannon balls, so I left him to face them alone, whilst I sloped a little to the right, and then fell in with Sir Edward Barnes, shot through the shoulder, supported in his saddle by his *aide-de-camp*, who begged me to go off to the nearest cavalry, and request that a man might be sent to assist in taking the general to the rear.

Barnes seeming faint from loss of blood, I drew forth my "pocket pistol," as it is termed, and offered him a little of the *liqueur* with which it was charged, which he at first declined, but afterwards accepted. I then obtained a horse artilleryman, whose help was urgently needed. Barnes was a noble officer in action— quite a fire-eater; he wore that day his full embroidered uniform, which rendered him very conspicuous, as all the rest of the staff were in blue undress coats, or rather showed nothing but cloaks, as a drizzling rain prevailed till the afternoon.[3]

It will readily be understood that a junior like myself could be lit-

3. Hardly correct. The rain cleared off about 11 a.m.

tle more than a spectator generally: indeed, save that I carried two or three messages, I had really nothing to do during the day; my chief. Delancey, having been mortally wounded, although he lived for a day or two after the battle, no one troubled himself to notice me, so I rode about as I pleased. I think it was after seven o'clock that perfect stillness reigned on our front, and I, in my ignorance, fancying we were to have no more attacks, thought I would take a look in the rear of our left, in order to see if our friends the Prussians, who all day had been anxiously expected, were approaching; while riding towards the village of Ohain I heard guns at a distance on my right hand, but not many—probably the first that were fired against the enemy at Planchenoit.

Continuing my ride, I saw, some way off, a body of cavalry approaching, which proved to be Prussians, and soon came upon some infantry in skirmishing order; when, observing an officer, I advanced and spoke to him. He told me he was preceding the corps of General von Röder, and the general himself came in view at that moment, near enough for me to recognise him—having seen him before at Brussels; he, however, took no notice of me; so, after remaining a few minutes, observing the slow advance of the skirmishers, which to me seemed intolerable, knowing how ardently our allies had been expected to take part in the battle, and telling the officer I had spoken to that the British army was holding its ground, but greatly needed support, I retraced my steps.[4] My looking for the Prussians had taken some time, for my horse, rather fagged as well as wounded, carried me at a slow pace. On my way back the firing had increased near Planchenoit, a sound I was glad to hear.

Meanwhile important events had taken place, which I was deeply grieved to have missed. The final French attack had been repulsed, and when I got back to the crest of our position, I found it unoccupied, and our troops at the moment could be seen mounting the slope on the other side of the valley. Hurrah, the battle was gained! Of course I hastened on, making for the *chaussée* towards La Belle Alliance, but soon found it completely blocked by French guns and tumbrils, heaped upon each other in a mass of confusion; and, on getting to the top of the sloping ground, close to the farm of Rossomme, came to

---

4. These statements are evidence that Gneisenau carefully restrained the Prussian advance where it would relieve Wellington. Gneisenau distrusted the Duke, and was for some time uncertain whether he really had determined to fight at Waterloo.— See Rose's *Napoleon*, 2. 489.

a spot where many hundreds of French muskets lay in quite regular order, as if they had been put down by word of command; one of the farm buildings was in flames, and the lurid glare, defining the outlines of abandoned guns, fully horsed, gleaming too on the bright row of muskets, presented a striking scene, worthy the pencil of an artist.

Of course I did not linger there; crossing to the left of the *chaussée*, I found myself involved with Prussian infantry, streaming from the direction of Frischermont, in no military order whatever, as they swept onward bayoneting every wounded Frenchman they came upon. Seeing a knot of them standing close to a wall, I rode up and perceived a wounded English light dragoon sitting against it, and there seemed to be some hesitation as to his fate, when I called out, "*Er ist ein Engländer*," upon which the men raised their bayonets, and the poor fellow was saved. The disorder of the Prussians I had got amongst was so great that I was glad to push on, and soon overtook our 52nd Regiment, and near it our glorious commander, but thinly attended, and heard an order given for all our people to keep to the right of the road, leaving it clear for the Prussians.

Very soon our bugles sounded the "halt," and the 52nd formed up in line, as quiet and orderly as if at the termination of a review. It was commanded by Colonel Colborne (afterwards Lord Seaton), a splendid soldier, who had greatly distinguished himself in the Peninsula. The Duke remained for a short time talking with Colborne, whilst I was doing the same with Northey, a young subaltern of the regiment, who gave me some interesting particulars about what has since been termed, and with truth, the "crisis of Waterloo." He said the Duke was close to his regiment just after the repulse of the last and most serious attack of the day, when two heavy columns all but gained the crest of our position; that the Duke was observed using his field telescope, but, as it seemed, nervously; for he kept sliding its tube in and out. Certainly it was a moment when even the Iron Duke might feel excited. I heard him say to Colborne, as he shook hands on departing, that he would endeavour to send some flour for his men. He then turned his horse towards Waterloo, followed by five persons only.

On nearing the farm of La Belle Alliance, a group of horsemen were seen crossing the fields on our right; on seeing them, the Duke left the road to meet them. They proved to be Marshal Blücher and his suite. The two great chiefs cordially shook hands, and were together about ten minutes; it was then so dark that I could not distinguish Blücher's features, and had to ask a Prussian officer whom the Duke was conversing with, although I was quite close to him at the time, but of course not near enough to hear what was said. On leaving Blücher, the Duke rode at a walk towards Waterloo. Darkness shrouded the spectacle of the dead and dying near La Haye Sainte; but the frequent snorting of our horses as they trod between them showed that the ground, so fiercely contested during the day, was very thickly strewed with bodies of the brave.

I may, just in allusion to the place of meeting of Wellington and Blücher, observe that much discrepancy exists among its chroniclers; and, indeed, the Duke himself has said that it was at Genappe. Now, of course, the statement of so insignificant an individual as the present writer cannot be supposed to carry any weight against such high authority in a matter of *opinion*; but this is one of *fact*, and most assuredly, when the Duke called "halt" that night, our most advanced troops were not within two miles of Genappe. "*Voilà l'histoire,*" as Henry IV. of France exclaimed, on receiving contradictory accounts of the same event from eyewitnesses.

Chapter 7

Waterloo

When the Duke reached Waterloo, the village clock had struck ten. During the ride back, which was at a walk, and may have taken from half to three quarters of an hour, I did not observe the Duke speak to any of his little suite; indeed, he was evidently sombre and dejected; and well might he be so, even after such a triumph, for death had been busy that day among his old and well-tried companions in many a well-fought field; hence, we may believe that he only yielded to the dictates of his heart, when, on the following day, he wrote: "The losses I have sustained have quite broken me down, and I have no feeling for the advantages we have gained." The few individuals who attended him, wore, too, rather the aspect of a little funeral train than that of victors in one of the most important battles ever fought. But, in truth, we were really a set of mourners, since all had left friends or associates, more or less valued, stretched upon that bloody field—how many we then knew not.

The little inn at Waterloo was chiefly used by waggoners engaged in transporting merchandise between France and Belgium; indeed, of stabling there was sufficient for an entire squadron, in an immense sort of barn, having mangers all round, leaving ample space in the middle for the large two-wheeled vehicles used in the traffic. This place was filled with horses of our foreigners, and I could see little prospect of finding room for my own, which was hungry, tired, and though severely wounded, was not disabled. By the aid of a kind Dutch sergeant, I was at length enabled to get him standing-room and a supply of hay. On entering the inn, I was rejoiced to meet my kind friend Colonel Torrens, whom I had not seen during the latter part of the battle; I had lost sight of him soon after his having had a very narrow escape, his horse's head having been completely smashed by a shower of grape shot; when, with the coolness of an old Peninsula man, though under a heavy fire, he had managed to disengage the saddle and bridle of the dead animal, which were speedily transferred to the horse of a trooper that had become riderless.

In the spacious common room of the inn we found three or four small tables laid for supper, and several foreign officers, looking hungry and impatient, sat awaiting its appearance, and loudly discussing the events of the day. One table was secured by Torrens, and a smoking stew soon placed thereon. At that moment a Dutch officer in a staff uniform came up, and, with many bows and apologies, begged leave to join us. I had not tasted food since early morning, and before we sat down fancied myself hungry, but not a morsel could I swallow; my stomach was in no condition to take food; the emotions of the day overcame all appetite; neither could my friend do justice to the stew; but our Dutchman was able to eat for all, at the same time amusing us by recounting his exploits. No wonder the enemy had been vanquished, when such a terrible fellow headed charge after charge made by the Dutch cavalry.

For some time we enjoyed drawing out the little braggadocio; but, weariness succeeding, we began to think of repose. Torrens told me he had reserved the room marked for Sir W. Delancey, and that I could have it, and, with the hope of a good night's sleep after a day of such anxiety, excitement, and fatigue, I sought my chamber. On entering it, a deep groan met my ear, and, raising my candle, I perceived a burly form stretched upon the bed, habited in a blue uniform, having his legs cased in what we call jockey boots, which caused me at once to recognise a French officer, as I had noticed during the day that remarkable style of military dress. I civilly asked the interloper how he came to be there; when, raising himself by a painful effort to a sitting position, and pointing to the back of his head, he said, "*Regardez, monsieur.*"

Advancing the light close to his head, I saw a fearful gash, seeming as if a portion of the skull had been cut out; the wound had bled profusely, masses of coagulated blood adhering to the hair, whilst the pillow and bed were in a horrid state. "For the love of heaven," said he, "pray procure me a glass of water, as I am dying of thirst, and feel very faint, having lain here several hours, and not a soul has been near me." I, of course, got him some water, which afforded much relief, and he then asked how the battle had gone, since his capture early in the action; I fancy that must have been after the repulse of d'Erlon [in his attack] upon Picton's division, about two o'clock, when our heavy cavalry made fearful havoc among the enemy's disordered masses, making a large number of prisoners, as I have mentioned Poor fellow! what an expression of grim despair his countenance assumed, when I informed him how we had routed our foe in his successive attacks, horse and foot, *Garde Imperiale* included. Gnashing his teeth, he uttered, "*Plutôt la mort;*" then, a moment after, adding philosophically, "*Cependant, nous avons eu nos triomphes, et l'on lutte en vain contre la destinée.*"

Compassionating the man's wretched condition, I obtained warm water and tenderly washed his wound; I also got him a basin of *bouillon*, and indeed did all I could to make him as comfortable as circumstances permitted, for which he showered upon me every grateful expression the French vocabulary supplies, assuring me *le Capitaine le Maire* would thenceforth look upon every Englishman as a brother. Bidding him goodnight, I returned to the common room, intending to roll myself in my cloak and select a soft plank in the floor as a bed; but, unhappily, several foreigners sat drinking and noisily discussing the events of the battle, each, of course, claiming for his own countrymen the glory of it. Among them was a little Dutchman, who shone pre-eminent upon tactics, regarding which, as a staff officer, he was qualified to pronounce *ex cathedrâ*.

Unobserved by the noisy party. I lay down in a corner, but sleep was out of the question; as over-excitement had deprived me of appetite, so now it kept me awake; till length, the voices in the room becoming more and more indistinct, I gradually sank into a state of unconsciousness. An appalling dream succeeded, in which I beheld the chief incidents of the battle in distorted forms. There were furious attacks, and triumphant shouts as our battalions were overwhelmed. In the midst of a vast mass of fugitives, who, strangely enough, belonged to the enemy's Imperial Guard, I was flying to seek shelter in the forest, when a shot killed my horse, and in an instant I found myself in the powerful grasp of *Captain le Maire,* who, raising his sword, cried in a voice of thunder, "*Scélérat, reçois la mort en paiement de tes mensonges.*"

The gleam of his blade caught my eye as I cast on him a look of reproach; but just as the infuriate and ungrateful wretch was about to plunge it into my breast, his brawny frame was suddenly transformed into the slender figure of Colonel Torrens, and I heard him pronounce my name. Relieved from the terror of instant death, I began to breathe freely, and, endeavouring to collect my scattered senses, asked the cause of his visit; when he told me he had just been with the Duke, who had given him an order for the army to move forward He then said that I must be on the field at daybreak, and show the order to every officer holding any command; and "Here," said he, "is the Duke's memorandum," putting into my hand half a sheet of foolscap, containing but three lines, as follows:—

Memorandum.—The troops belonging to the allied army will move upon Nivelles at daylight.
(Signed)   Wellington.

"You will understand," continued the colonel, "that you must be careful to show, and, when necessary, interpret, the order to our foreign leaders; you are, in fact, to act as a sort of whipper-in, and don't forget to arouse the skulkers in the wood."

It was then past one, and as I was to be on the ground before three o'clock, any more sleep was not to be thought of; besides, I wanted to see my horse, and ascertain whether the wound had rendered him unfit for work. I had some trouble to find the hostler, who lay snoring beneath a manger, and no little difficulty in getting him to move when discovered; however, the old resource—bribery—had its usual effect, and the man became at once as active as a horse-booth keeper at Epsom on the Derby Day. The injury to my horse was in the lower part of the belly, a ball having passed between the skin and ribs for a distance, as ascertained afterwards, of about eighteen inches, without causing a very dangerous wound. The parts adjacent were much swollen, but the animal did not seem in pain, so I prescribed a feed of oats, and by two o'clock was in the saddle, on my way to the field; the shades of night being rendered doubly dark by the lofty trees of the forest.

By the way, on visiting that locality many years afterwards, I found the trees had been cleared away between Waterloo and Mont St Jean, and I had a difficulty in recognising the locality as it was in 1815.

Being rather before my time, I rode at a walk, musing, as I advanced in the darkness, on the momentous events of the last three days, in which I felt proud to have borne a humble part. I was weary, too, and drowsy, sufficient to "steep my senses in forgetfulness," and felt a doubt of the reality of all I had witnessed, fancying the battle, the defeat of the enemy, their flight, with our pursuit, might after all be only a series of dreamy delusions. But as the fall of our book, when we sink into a dozing state, immediately restores our faculties, so on that occasion, a trip of my steed brought back my wandering senses; and the outlines of the farm buildings of La Haye Sainte, traced before me in the gloom, served to satisfy me that all was not a dream.

As I passed those walls, riddled by cannon shot, around which there had been such fierce strife, such daring valour exhibited on one side, and determined resolution on the other; and when, moreover, I imagined myself the sole human being capable of movement over ground, whereon thousands and thousands of brave men, dead, dying, and suffering, were at that moment lying, who but a few short hours before were full of health and vigour, I felt deeply awe-stricken, and though not then of an age to moralise profoundly, my reflections were more philanthropic than soldier-like, more creditable to my feelings than to my ambition.

What desolation unfolded itself as the light increased! Every vestige of crops had disappeared, the ground looking like a vast fallow, strewed with the wrecks of a mighty army—nay, I may say of armies; for, if the presence around of an abundance of cannon, muskets, and other *débris*, together with the bodies of the fallen, attested the utter ruin of the French, I had but to look across the wide valley to behold enough of what the historian of the Peninsular War, Napier, terms, the "blood and bones" of the British, to make it clear that Wellington could have no very imposing army left; and might exclaim, with Pyrrhus, "Such another victory, and we are undone." A shallow, hollow way, as the road rises towards the position of the French, I found completely blocked by guns and tumbrils packed and wedged together, and. indeed, pitched topsy-turvy one upon another, many having evidently rolled down the banks, some ten feet high; the space occupied by this confused mass was about fifty yards, and may be likened to the appearance which a railway presents after a tremendous smash. I counted twenty guns.

The Duke says in his despatch that on the repulse of the last great attack, he ordered the whole of his troops to advance, but I had the means of seeing that all did not move forward, for two small 2nd battalions, namely, of the 33rd and 69th regiments, did not get beyond Hougomont. Having suffered severely at Quatre Bras, they had been united to form one battalion, and when posted near our centre on the 18th, had come in for more than their share of the fighting. When the Imperial Guard made the last grand attack of the day, a withering fire (even when united, it formed but a weak battalion) was poured in; its Commander and numbers fell, its array was broken, and confusion ensued; but the efforts of the brave Colonel Muttlebury, of the 69th,

46

rallied the men, and they gallantly kept their ground. But physical power has its limits, and the same men who had rallied at a trying and critical moment, were wholly unable to move forward and take part in the pursuit of the enemy. I found the poor fellows, a wretched remnant, bivouacked under the trees of Hougomont, preparing to bury the bodies of their fallen comrades.

It may readily be understood that the duty on which I was employed afforded me ample means of seeing the state of things just as the darkness had left them the night before, and such as no other person could observe, since I alone, as bearer of the Duke's order, had to visit every part. Of course, I first sought out the leaders of the British troops, and then those of our allies.[1] Here and there I came upon little shelters, which had been hastily prepared to screen some officer of rank who had been wounded, consisting of a couple of blankets, or some other slight covering; but they were few, as generally the soldiers managed to transport their wounded officers to the rear.

As, I believe, no provisions had reached the troops, I had to listen to remonstrances against marching on empty stomachs; but there was no help for it, move they must, and very soon most of them began to march across the fields in the direction of the Nivelles road, the men, as may be imagined, looking haggard, with uniforms soiled by lying on the wet ground, and in all respects wearing a very different aspect from that of the trim soldiers as seen at home.

When I had finished my mission, and was returning to make my report, I chanced to fall in with a small party of a Hanoverian Hussar regiment, and, on addressing its commander, he told me his soldiers were in no condition to march, that the regiment had been almost annihilated, and that those with him, numbering some 140 men, were all that remained of 800. Much as I felt for a commander so circumstanced, I could do no more than express my sympathy, and regret that, the order for all to march being imperative, he had no option. I afterwards learned that this regiment had declined to share in the conflict, and had gone off almost bodily to the forest. The men were in some sort volunteers, finding their own horses and equipments, and belonged generally to a superior class of society to that whence sol-

---

1. In the *Autobiography* of Sir Harry Smith we read (1. 274); "Before daylight next morning (19th June) a staff officer, whose name I now forget, rode up to where we were all lying and told us of the complete *déroute* of the French, and the vigorous pursuit of the Prussians, and that it was probable that our Division would not move for some hours." There is little doubt that this staff officer was Lieutenant Jackson.

diers are usually drawn.[2] When we succeed in inducing a better class of men to engage in our own ranks, let us hope for a better result.

Early that morning, two troops of our spring waggons, forty-eight in number, came up from Brussels, the captain in command telling me his orders were to follow the army; and they were about to file off in the direction of Nivelles, when the chief medical officer of our army urged the propriety and necessity of at once getting up the wounded. Some hesitation occurred as to how the Captain ought to act, when the Duke rode up and directed that every waggon should remain until all the wounded were picked up. Before night, I believe that all the British wounded were removed from the ground, and lodged under such shelter as Mont St Jean and Waterloo afforded, where the medical staff had, little or no rest, whether by day or night, for upwards of a week.

I remember seeing in published accounts, that the wounded of our allies, and also those of the French, were brought in indiscriminately with our own. Very philanthropic and praiseworthy it sounded, but I much fear we cannot claim such a stretch of humanity. The truth is, that, as far as our means allowed, the wounded of the British and "King's German Legion" were first thought of, and then those of the Hanoverians. The Brunswickers, Dutch, and Belgians, all had *ambulances*, or hospital waggons, for the use of their own wounded; but the French were left for the waggons of the country to gather in, and the poor fellows, being in great numbers, lay long on the ground; this was very sad, as it was only on the fourth day after the battle that the last were got in.

It is painful to think of their sufferings from pain, cold, and even hunger, during so many weary days and nights: numbers indeed must have perished who would have lived, could they have received care and surgical attention. No food was supplied to them save what the peasant women, who went about with pitchers of water and bread, were able to afford, the humble offering of true Christian charity. The villages and hamlets adjacent received the French, who filled the churches, barns, and outhouses, each little community clubbing contributions of meat, bread, and vegetables, to make soup for their sustenance.

The bodies of the slain were stripped in an incredibly short time,

---

2. This was the Cumberland regiment of Hanoverian Hussars (volunteers). See Siborne, *The Waterloo Campaign*, pp. 464, 465; also Professor Oman in the *Nineteenth Century* for October 1900.

becoming in the course of a few days horrible objects; those lying exposed to the sun turning nearly black, as well as being much swollen; while such as lay around Hougomont, partially shaded by its trees, retained their natural whiteness. Not aware of the shocking sights offered by a battlefield, a party of English ladies and gentlemen visited the ground from Brussels, but a single glance so shocked our fair countrywomen, as to make them fly away like scared doves.

To clear the ground of dead men and horses occupied ten or twelve days, which disgusting duly was performed by the peasantry. The human bodies were thrown into large holes, fifteen or twenty feet square, while those of the animals were honoured with a funeral pile and burned, their carcasses, many of which became inflated to an enormous size, being dragged with great labour to the heaps of faggots. The officer in command of the Royal Waggon Train, who furnished me with the above details, also narrated an incident creditable to the feelings and fidelity of an English soldier. The man had been servant to Sir Henry Ellis, who commanded the 23rd Fusiliers, a distinguished officer, and had remained behind, in order to find the body of his master; having succeeded, he applied to my informant for assistance to bury it, urging that it would be discreditable to allow any but English hands to render that service to his honoured master. His request was complied with, and four British soldiers carried Sir Henry's body, and laid it in the churchyard of Braine L'Alleud.

Many years afterwards, on mentioning the circumstance to Colonel Enoch, then employed at the Horse Guards, he told me that he was adjutant of the 23rd at Waterloo, and how Sir Henry, before the action began, called all his officers around him, and told them that it was his positive order that no man should fall out of the ranks to assist any one wounded, whether officer or soldier, and that the order comprised himself as well as others. On receiving a musket ball in his side, he quietly left the square alone, and was seen to fall from his horse soon after. Such was the discipline of the regiment, that his orders were strictly obeyed, and he was left where he fell. It was thought in the regiment, that if succoured immediately, his valuable life might possibly have been saved.

CHAPTER 8

The Battlefield

It was past midday ere I felt myself at liberty to leave the field, for up to that hour soldiers continued to appear in small bodies, seeking their regiments, numbers of our foreigners emerging from the forest. The hamlet of Mont St Jean then presented a bustling scene as the wounded arrived there, while troops, guns, and waggons with stores of ammunition and provisions came up from Brussels, taking the direction of Nivelles, the road to which, branching off to the right from Mont St Jean, in a word, the high road, presented a complete reflux of the tide that had ebbed so hastily the day before.

Death in every varied form had by this time become so familiar to me, that I scarcely noticed the bodies which lay in my way, but I felt a sickening sensation on seeing the remains of a Brunswick soldier, apparently quite a lad, lying partly buried in the mire on the high road. A heavy wheel must have passed over his head. crushing it flat, and scattering the brains. This was at Mont St Jean, but no one thought of pulling the body aside from the road, any more than one would think of withdrawing a dead cat or dog from the street.

We read that in the East there prevails a degree of indifference both to human life and suffering which we, in our more advanced civilisation, feel shocked at; but such is the ductile nature of man, that habit can reconcile him to almost anything; and I verily believe that, after another battle or two, even such a sight as the pyramid of heads, which we are told was raised in front of the Emperor Baber's tent, would have had no more effect upon me than it probably had upon a staff officer of Baber. However that might be, I was glad to depart from the sad scene in my, as yet, only semi-barbarised state, and betake myself to the Waterloo hostelry, that I might obtain refreshment, the morning's exercise, after a fast of six-and-thirty hours, having sharpened my appetite to a painful extent. My poor nag, too, seeming spurred by a pleasing idea of oats and hay, soon took me to its door.

Having made a report of my mission, and partaken of some food. I bethought me of the wounded *Captain le Maire*, so I tapped at the door of his chamber, and, receiving no response, opened it, and entered; but lo! the bird had flown. The people of the inn said he had disappeared, but further knew nothing. Possibly his wound, though fearful to look at, may not have prevented his stealing into the friendly forest for concealment, and finally escaping to France.

My next object was to go to Brussels, and see after my two servants, horses, and effects; and, having obtained the necessary permission from my immediate superior, I started, and, notwithstanding the somewhat enfeebled condition of my wounded horse, was soon in the city, where I found numbers of wounded men, and many, I believe, with whole skins, chiefly Prussians from Ligny, lying in the streets, to whom the kind inhabitants were distributing food. I found the place in considerable disorder, but thought that a great battle fought so near sufficiently accounted for this. Little did I then imagine that a panic had reigned the day before, owing to a report, generally credited, that we were defeated, and in full retreat. On reaching my quarters, what was my surprise to find the horses jaded and covered with mud, and my two fellows wisping them with great vigour. On my angrily enough demanding an explanation, one of them said, "We are only just come back from Antwerp."

"But what on earth took you to Antwerp?"

"Why, we were told the battle was lost, and the French coming in, and so we thought it best to do like the rest"

"Well, and what made you return? "I asked.

"Well, we were no sooner inside the ramparts of Antwerp, than we heard it was a false alarm, and we returned."

So my nags had been all night upon the road, and travelled fifty miles, because the men took fright.

Of the English families then at Brussels, there was one with which in after years my dearest interests became identified,[8] When Colonel Muttlebury marched with his regiment on the 16th, his wife and two little girls remained in the city; and the condition of the poor lady may well be conceived on the afternoon of that day, when a tremendous cannonade arose. I have already said how terribly distinct the

---

1. Colonel Jackson married a daughter of Colonel Muttlebury.

51

firing at Quatre Bras and Ligny resounded in the city, and the alarm it caused, especially in the breast of one who knew her husband must be engaged.

It was not till about midday of the 17th. when our wounded began to arrive, that anything became known of the fighting. Descrying from her window the uniform of her husband's regiment, Mrs Muttlebury rushed into the street, and learned from the mouth of a soldier, that It had been hotly engaged, and had suffered severe loss, but that when he left it, the colonel was still unhurt. In the course of the day came a couple of lines, pencilled upon a drum head, from himself. Thus relieved, the anxious lady was tranquillised for the night, thinking that probably the strife was all over.

Heavy clouds and rain ushered in the morning of the 18th, fit emblems of the tears that dreadful day was destined to call forth; it was the Sabbath, too; and what a day for wholesale slaughter of the Creator's image! Once more the roar of cannon struck terror to the heart of Mrs Muttlebury, as she clasped her children to her breast, and taught them to pray for the preservation of their father. Then there was hurrying through the street—cries of alarm, and her landlady rushed in, shrieking out that the French were at the gates, and she must try and hide the terrorised little group, or her own life would be forfeited, because she had harboured English persons. Her own dastardly man- servant had fled, and the misery of the poor lady attained its climax. But religion, the Christian's blessed anchor, lent its support; she sought her prayer-book, and read the Lessons and Psalms for the day; and found consolation in the ninety-first Psalm:

He shall defend thee under His wings, and thou shalt be safe under His feathers; His faithfulness and truth shall be thy shield and buckler.

Again, in the seventh verse:

A thousand shall fall beside thee, and ten thousand at thy right hand; but it shall not come nigh thee.

She clung to these assurances, as an omen from on high, addressed specially to her case; they inspired a holy confidence that her dear husband would be spared. Towards evening, a great commotion was heard, and an English staff officer appeared in the street, waving his cocked-hat, and calling out words which the uproar drowned. At length Mrs Muttlebury caught the words, "The French, here they come;" and verily there they came; not, however, as victors flushed with conquest, but as miserable dejected creatures, mostly bareheaded, bleeding, and with soiled and rent garments, unhappy prisoners, in numbers perhaps 2000; the same whom I had seen marched off after the failure of the first attack on Picton's division, as I have mentioned A feeble detachment of Dutch infantry, not more than 160 strong, sufficed to escort and control so large a body of dejected men.

The arrival of the prisoners, about six o'clock, marching through the principal streets, tended greatly to allay the general trepidation, though the continuance of firing plainly told that the battle still raged. By dawn next morning, however, news of our victory arrived, and while Mrs Muttlebury. agitated by anxiety, dread, suspense, and hope, was awaiting intelligence of her husband, he himself, begrimed with the stains of battle, and exhausted by hunger and fatigue, rushed into the room; and the ecstasy of one long embrace sufficed to efface in both the remembrance of all past suffering.

But let me return to my own little proceedings. The state of my horses, after the wayward run of my men to Antwerp, precluded all idea of immediately following the army; so I was fain to remain for the night in the city. On the fallowing morning, early (the 20th), I started, having my servants and baggage with me, not daring to trust them again out of my sight. On reaching Mont St Jean, I saw a goodly show of captured guns ranged near a large farm building, and stopped to count them—one hundred and thirty-three pieces; I had expected to find more, as we had formed a very large estimate of the enemy's artillery.

In after years the discrepancy was thus accounted for. I had the pleasure of knowing Sir Alexander Dickson, the excellent officer who had been in chief command of the artillery in the Peninsula; and, when conversing with him about Waterloo and the French guns, he asked if I had ever heard what took place respecting them. He then told me that on the day after the battle, meeting Sir George Wood, who commanded our artillery, he asked whether steps had been taken to collect the captured pieces. Sir George said he had not given the matter a thought, but would have it seen to. Accordingly, parties of the artillery were ordered for the purpose, but no guns could be found, all having disappeared from the field. This was a pretty business, and Sir George had nothing for it but to inform the Duke. His Grace, usually so calm, flew into a towering passion, frightening poor Sir George out of his wits; and well he might storm, upon losing so many solid trophies of his victory; and ended by swearing by the guns must be found.

Meanwhile a report had come in that the Prussians, on the allied army marching off, had gone over the ground in considerable numbers, and in a surprisingly short time taken away every piece to Genappe. A captain of artillery was then sent to remonstrate and see what could be done to recover our legitimate spoil, and in the end he was lucky enough to persuade the Prussian Commander to deliver up one-half of the guns in his possession; so the French had two hundred and sixty-six pieces present on the 18th June.[2] What proportion had been turned against the Prussians at Planchenoit, no one can say; but any captured there, belonged, of course, to them; still, the lion's share was properly ours—perhaps not less than two hundred guns. However, as things turned out, we were fortunate in bagging one hundred and thirty-three. The Prussians were thus sad rogues in those days, both wholesale and retail, as I have now recorded, à propos of horses as well as cannon. Let me add, that not a whisper of this affair of the guns was breathed by our prudent artillery—at least, none ever reached me while I remained with the army. I afterwards found it recorded In the published journal of General Mercer, who commanded a troop of horse artillery in the battle. His little book is full of interesting details.

In order to take a last view of the well-fought field, I turned off the road on leaving Mont St Jean and rode along the crest of our position. It being the first appearance of my fresh horse upon battle ground, he snorted and shied at the bodies, and I had some difficulty to get him past them; they were then lying where they had fallen, none having been removed; but when I came to the place, or rather places, where the wounded and dead of the Imperial Guard lay, almost on the crest of our position, on the right, near Hougomont, the animal's fears abated, and he consented to approach them. I talked with two or three of the poor fellows, who differed in the accounts they gave as to how they had been overthrown: one said cavalry had charged them, another that it was infantry; in fact, they seemed bewildered. As they lay, they formed large squares, of which the centres were "hollow." Several endeavoured to attract my notice, saying they had been left for two days unheeded, and beseeching me to try and get them removed.

One would call out. "Ah, *mon officier,* I suffer dreadfully from hunger, cold, and my wound;" another would pray, "*Monsieur le Capitaine*"

2. Dr J. Holland Rose in his recent *Life of Napoleon* (2, 493) says that Napoleon had 246 cannon against 156 of the Allies. The figure 246 for Napoleon is founded on the very careful estimate in Houssaye's *Waterloo,* (also published by Leonaur.)

to have "*pitié de lui;*" while a third begged *Monsieur le Colonel* to do something for him— this with a twinkle of the eye, when addressing a boy of twenty years. I did not await further promotion; but said *bon jour* to the brave fellows, with an expression of regret, that, being merely a powerless subaltern, I could do nothing for them. I have generally found in the French soldier, a pleasant, lively, and shrewd fellow; and many a talk I have had with him in the course of my rambles about his country, deriving therefrom both amusement and information.

On overtaking my servants, I asked why they had not paused for a few minutes to view the field; when my factotum, a sturdy little Welshman, standing some five feet nothing, though a soldier, told me he had no taste for such a sight, and was, moreover, unwilling to fatigue the horses by going off the road. "But," said I, "you don't object to overloading them by adding this," drawing forth from my baggage two huge French cavalry sabres from the load of a little Cossack horse. "Oh," said little Taffy, "they are for our defence when we get into France."

Chapter 9

A Review

I must now permit myself to make a few brief observations upon this important battle. Of the numerous incidents it presents, it strikes me that the repulse of Count d'Erlon's formidable attack on the 18th, early in the day, upon Picton's weak division, is the one most deserving of our admiration. To form a just opinion of Picton's nerve, judgement, and decision, we must remember that, to meet the onset of three columns, amounting to 13,000 bayonets, we had only 3000 British infantry—all that remained of the 4600 with whom he had borne the brunt of the severe action of Quatre Bras; that a Dutch brigade, originally posted in his front, fled almost before the enemy came within musket shot; and further, that he had no troops whatever behind him as a reserve in case of disaster. The maintenance of, perhaps, our entire position, depended on the ability of 3000 men, formed only two deep, to drive back three massive columns, each of which far exceeded the strength of his own.

Preceded, as usual, by a cloud of skirmishers, and covered by the fire of sixty or seventy pieces of cannon pealing across the valley, which told with effect, d'Erlon's columns came steadily on, notwithstanding the fire of our guns, which played upon them, until they got within long musket range of the Dutch, who, as I have already said, fled to the rear; and the French could then see no opponents before them, the British having been kept just under the brow of the rising ground. But on the instant, when, at a distance of some fifty or sixty yards, the enemy halted, and began to deploy into line, Picton moved up Kempt's Brigade to a straggling hedge running along that part, helping to conceal our men, which poured a withering fire upon the enemy, followed by a charge with the bayonet.

Having but a moment to glance at the unexpected foe, unable to form any estimate of his strength, while hidden by the smoke, staggered by so sudden and unexpected a fire, confounded, panic-stricken, the French fell into immediate confusion, broke, and fled. The second column, being treated in a similar manner, followed suit; and the brigade of British heavy cavalry dashing down the slope under Ponsonby, in the midst of their confusion, the enemy had not a chance of rallying under the sabres of the dragoons, and over 2000 were captured. Would that the gallant Picton could have seen the glorious success of his daring! A musket shot hit him in the temple at the moment he gave the word to charge, and he fell dead upon the spot.

To make the non-military reader comprehend how such large bodies of good infantry could be so speedily disposed of by one weak division, I may be allowed to say a few words upon the columnar mode of attack, generally successful when practised by the French, until they tried it against the British troops.

The system is as old as the Macedonian *phalanx*, and had been more or less followed at various periods by most continental nations, up to the time of Gustavus Adolphus; but that great commander, perceiving the folly of placing a body of men in a situation to prevent them from using their firearms, caused his Swedes to attack in line. Marlborough, Frederick, and others confirmed by their practice the opinion of Gustavus; but the undisciplined armies of the French Revolution abandoned that order of combat, relying on the moral effect of rapidly pushing forward large masses against the weakest parts of an enemy's position—a method that rarely failed of success against continental armies; for, impelled by natural ardour and enthusiasm, they dashed on with the *élan* for which they have credit, and actually frightened the defenders by their rapid and imposing advance.

The least reflection must satisfy any one, that, while massed in close columns, an enemy is really only formidable to the imagination: for, as the foremost ranks mask all those behind them, it is only from a narrow front that fire can be given first; and before the entire body can be brought to act physically, that is, by using their muskets, the manoeuvre of deploying, or forming into line, must be resorted to, which is commonly begun from the rear, the *front* maintaining a fire to cover the operation.

Now there is nothing which so greatly discomposes troops as volleys of musketry poured in during such an evolution; and, if instantaneously followed by a determined bayonet charge, their defeat becomes inevitable. No one knew this better than Picton, who had seen many formidable-looking columns so driven off in the Peninsula; and when those of d'Erlon came on, in what the Duke calls the "old style," relying on the steadiness and pluck of his own men, he felt confident the enemy would be "driven off in the old style."

At Waterloo, the French had a fine opportunity of wiping out the stain of their Peninsula defeats. Numerically, the armies opposed to each other were nearly equal; but how differently were they composed! Napoleon's force consisted of his old Imperial soldiers, while Wellington commanded a motley body, as we have seen; and, moreover, most of the foreigners were, as I have said, young soldiers, who had never before seen a shot fired. Again, a large portion of the allied army was not present, having been posted in the vicinity of Hal, some miles distant, the Duke fearing an effort to turn his right at that point—a disposition of his force much criticised, especially by General Count von Gneisenau, the chief of Blücher's staff; and, if I may be permitted to give my humble opinion, I think the criticism not unreasonable. Be that as it may, the arrangement deprived the Duke of a goodly portion of his army, when all were much needed in the conflict. My own estimate is, that he had no more than from 18,000 to 20,000 infantry actually present on whom he could place reliance. Then the French cavalry far outnumbered the British, and the enemy's guns were ninety in excess of our own.

The French soldiers are, perhaps, as brave as our own, but their courage is of a different kind: our men like to come to close quarters with their opponents, whereas the French prefer keeping at a reasonable distance, preferring the report of a musket to the gleam of the bayonet; in equal numbers they are a match for the soldiers of most nations, and are on the whole excellent troops, but difficult to keep within the rules of discipline.

In all their battles the French have shown much predilection for attacking and defending posts and villages, and, adhering to this practice, Napoleon spent the entire afternoon of the 16th in assailing St Amand and Ligny, both of which were carried after many severe struggles and great loss: it is true they lie in the low ground, and in front of Blücher's position, and hence it could not be attacked in that part till those villages were taken; but it is questionable whether Napoleon ought not to have made his greatest efforts upon the extreme right of Blücher, when, if successful, he would have cut off the communication between the Prussians and British, driving the former towards Namur, and preventing all possibility of the latter receiving Prussian support.

Again, at Waterloo, the first attack was upon Hougomont, a country house with outbuildings, which had to sustain several severe attacks; but all were repulsed. The little wood close to the house was occupied at first by Nassau troops, who soon disappeared, leaving the defence of the house and out-buildings to a detachment of our Guards, who gallantly held the post. Seeing the importance attached to it by the enemy, the Duke, after the first grand onset by Jerome Bonaparte, sent thither a strong reinforcement, which rendered it perfectly secure. It appears to me, that to penetrate Wellington's left centre, and thereby render himself master of the *chaussée* to Brussels by Mont St Jean, should have been Napoleon's great object; as, if successful, he would have cut off our communication with the Prussian army. Had such been his tactics, and (the attack made at the same moment when Jerome assailed Hougomont, and made, moreover, with his best troops, *viz.*, the Imperial Guard, it might have gone hard with us. The object, then, of the Hougomont attack should have been considered of secondary importance, and chiefly with a view to preventing Wellington from weakening his right in order to strengthen his left centre.[1]

There has been much controversy respecting the amount and value of the Prussian co-operation at Waterloo. For myself. I think it not unlikely that several causes produced delay in their reaching our field. First, we must recollect the defeat of Ligny, and that a beaten army is always differently actuated from a successful one. Secondly, the road between Wavre and the field of Waterloo had been rendered very bad by recent rain; and thirdly, not knowing that Wellington had great difficulty in maintaining his position at Quatre Bras, the Prussian Generals may have resented the non-assistance of the British at their battle, as they had been led to expect. The extreme deliberation of their approach by Ohain I have before pointed out; and I may here mention that, In talking over this with Captain Siborne, whose history of the campaign, I think, evidences Prussian proclivity—he was of German descent—he admitted that our ally ought to have been up sooner.

As regards Napoleon, it must be allowed that his difficulties were great. Amongst his generals, he seems to have not known whom to trust. It is clear he feared Soult, the best of them, and so kept him near his person, with no command;[2] then Ney, brave, but with no head,

---

1. Napoleon at first only intended the attack on Hougomont to be a diversion, his main object all along being to pierce Wellington's left centre. The Hougomont attack became severe and protracted owing to the persistent folly of Jerome Bonaparte.

The Farm of Hougomont after the Battle of Waterloo

only joined the very day the Sambre was crossed, taking command of a *corps d'armée* destined to assail Wellington. In his zeal confidence might be placed, as he would fight with a halter round his neck, after the treachery of Grenoble. Lastly, Grouchy tells us that, on the morning of the 17th, instead of following close on the heels of Blücher's retreat, he was engaged walking to and fro with Napoleon near Ligny talking of the state of parties at Paris! Did the Emperor distrust him, in dread lest, like Judas, he might betray his master? Surely we need feel no surprise at Napoleon's *méfiance* of his chief men, when we recollect that de Bourmont, his Chief of the Staff, deserted to the Prussians just before the passage of the Sambre. He, however, did not remain with them, but came on to us, and was for the greater part of the 18th riding with the headquarters staff—a conspicuous figure, wearing a bright *cuirass*.

I have mentioned being employed in examining and reporting upon various roads leading from Brussels towards the French frontier, and that one of my reports touched upon the little River Dyle, naming the bridges spanning it at Wavre, Limale, and Limelette. The report also described the nature of the road running from Wavre through the village of Gembloux to the point of its junction with the *chaussée* leading from Quatre Bras to Namur. As the Prussians retreated, after Ligny, by this route, and subsequently skirted the Dyle when moving from Wavre to unite with us at Waterloo, it is possible that a British subaltern may have rendered some service to our gallant allies. I know that the said report was transmitted to Count Gneisenau, Blücher's Chief of the Staff.[3] Now for our march to Paris. I reached Nivelles on the evening of the 20th, and thence proceeding by Mons, rejoined headquarters at Le Cateau on the 22nd, taking care not to lose sight of my baggage.

---

2. In this paragraph Colonel Jackson falls into serious error. Soult, so far from having no command, was Chief of the General Staff of the French army in this campaign, and signed all Napoleon's orders. On the other hand de Bourmont was only General of Division, and commanded the 14th Division of Infantry, which was in the corps of Gerard. See Houssaye's *Waterloo*. Again, it is suggested that on the morning of the 17th Napoleon distrusted Grouchy. It is clear, however, that Napoleon did not distrust him at 11 a.m. of this day, or he would not have given him so important a command and mission. Napoleon's delay on this morning was due to his belief that he had crushed the Prussians, who were, he thought, making for Namur or in that direction, and also to his ignorance—up to 11 a.m.—that Wellington was still clinging to Quatre Bras. See Rose's *Napoleon*, 2.481.

3. See remark on this in my Introduction.

On the way, I fell into company with some French officers, of the suite of Louis XVIII., who had come from Ghent, where that monarch sojourned, after his expulsion from the Tuileries. They talked much and loud, had a swaggering air, looking like conquerors. Two or three Belgian officers were of the party. One of them, who had evidently been in the French service, discoursed to me upon their great superiority in the art of war, saying, "*I'l faut convenir qu'ils sont en tout nos maîtres.*" To which I replied, that we English had received instruction in a very agreeable manner, seeing the pupils had on all occasions beaten their masters. This rejoinder dearly gave offence, as the Belgian assumed a sulky aspect, and said not another word.

CHAPTER 10

Paris

On entering France, I was surprised to find the peasantry ignorant of the French language, speaking only an incomprehensible *patois*, not then being aware how little French is spoken in their class, throughout the length and breadth of the land, most provinces having their *patois*, used by them, the better classes only speaking French.

During our march to the vicinity of Paris, few occurrences came under my notice worthy of mention. The people were everywhere civil and obliging, and as they had no fear of molestation from us, everything went on as usual. I believe it was intended that the Prussian army should keep clear of the roads followed by the British; but this arrangement was not carefully carried out, for a body of Prussians during several days preceded us upon one route, to our great inconvenience; as at their approach the inhabitants of the villages fled, when our friends rifled every house; so that when we came up not a soul was to be seen, nor could the staff purchase an article of food.

It was sad to find cellars knee-deep with cider, the casks having been staved, and furniture and bedding destroyed, while, In many instances, we found houses burnt. The crops, too, suffered a good deal; for, not content to march upon the road, the troops often deviated from it, and moved over the adjacent fields, thereby treading down a belt of considerable width. All this, it is true, was only retaliating upon the French what their armies had done when masters in Prussia; and possibly we English, who felt pained at witnessing such wanton destruction, might have acted similarly under the like provocation.

We halted at the little town of Gonesse, about ten miles short of the capital, which continued our headquarters during the negotiation, which ended in the military convention of Paris. But after it was signed, the Prussians had some desultory fighting towards Versailles, which I saw from a height, having ridden out in that direction; or, speaking more correctly, I heard the reverberation of their guns among the fine scenery around St Cloud and Marly, which, with their smoke rising between the wooded hills, produced a fine effect

The convention was signed on the 3rd July, and on the following day Lieutenant-Colonel Torrens and Major Stavely, of the Royal Staff Corps, were despatched to Paris, as commissioners, to see it duly carried out by the French. I felt particularly desirous to go with them, and begged Torrens to ask permission to take me; but only two officers could be allowed to go; and a providential refusal it was, as will be seen. They started, escorted by a sinister-looking French officer, sent for that purpose, and to pass them through the advanced posts; an orderly dragoon attended them. They found the way barricaded at three several points, ere they reached the Faubourg St Denis, defensive lines having been raised against the hostile armies.

The French soldiers were in much disorder, scowling at the English officers as they passed, but this was no more than might be expected; when, however, they had got within the last barrier, the soldiers raised a tumult, and stopped them. Then a cry arose of *à bas les Anglais!* Some shots were fired, one of which killed the dragoon, Stavely receiving at the same moment a severe wound in the left side, being dragged from his horse; white Torrens, seeing no other chance of escape, drove the spurs into his horse and rapidly broke through the mob uninjured. The French officer, whose duty it was to protect those under his care, slunk away as soon as the affray became serious, and was no more seen.

Instead of being despatched, as he expected, Stavely was allowed to stagger into a *cabaret* close by, and seat himself in a room with many riotous half-drunken soldiers, some of whom menaced him by look and gesture, but refrained from otherwise molesting him, as he sat apart, leaning on a table, being weak from loss of blood. Meanwhile, Torrens galloped on, passing unchallenged into the city through the Porte St Denis, and, seeing an officer on reaching the Boulevards, he requested him to direct him to the residence of Davoust, who then commanded in Paris, whom he luckily found at home, and who, on being told of what had occurred, sent off an officer of rank to the scene of the affray; and Stavely, being found by him in the situation I have described, was immediately conveyed to Davoust's hotel. Such is the account I received from the lips of Torrens and Stavely, when we, a few days after, peaceably entered the capital. So, as I have said above,

I had a fortunate escape from an unexpected peril.

While the usual suspension of arms existed until the French should withdraw from Paris, (one day mounted into a windmill, standing on elevated ground near St Denis, and directly afterwards Lord Hill also ascended, to observe the French troops who remained close to that place, expecting to see them march off; we were near enough to see that they were making preparations for moving. I had not before met His Lordship, and was greatly struck with his urbanity and kind manner in questioning and talking to so young an officer as myself On leaving the mill I thoughtlessly proposed to a friend that we should ride down and see something of the soldiers as they were departing, thinking there was no fear of meeting with anything unpleasant, since hostilities were over. We were about to enter within the entrenchments at a part where an *abattis* had been removed, when we met Mackworth, one of Lord Hill's *aides-de-camp*, coming out in an excited state, who said, "Go back, unless you want to get into danger;" that he, having been sent with a message from Lord Hill to the officer in command of the French, had been surrounded and menaced by the soldiery, and esteemed himself fortunate in escaping from them.

Of course we had sense enough to take his advice, and retire. On the 5th of July our headquarters were transferred to Neuilly, and on the 7th the troops closed upon Paris, but none entered the city, a division being encamped in the Champs Elysées, others in the Bois de Boulogne, and cantoned in the neighbouring villages; the headquarters staff being quartered in Paris. I was allotted a *colonel's* billet on Monsieur Marchand, *Ordonnateur-en-chef* of the French armies, living in the Rue Neuve de Luxembourg. He received me very courteously, and provided accommodation for myself, servants, and horses, at an *hôtel garni* in the Rue St Honoré. He also invited me to dinner, asking whether I would meet his family and dine with them at three o'clock, or with him at six. I gallantly accepted the former proposition; but afterwards got a message putting me off till six, at which hour I found the family assembled, and was hospitably entertained.

The reason, perhaps, of meeting such civility at first may have arisen from my host's esteeming himself fortunate that a Prussian had not been quartered on him. He had held his important office under Napoleon, and was continued in it by Louis for some time, in order to organise the Department under the new *régime*. On taking my leave in the evening, Monsieur Marchand said he hoped to be favoured with my company at six, whenever it might suit my convenience to dine at his house. Considering this as merely politeness, I did not take it *au pied de la lettre*; but on the following day Monsieur Marchand called upon me, was very civil, hoped I found myself comfortably lodged, and ended by saying his family reckoned upon seeing me at six. His manner was so frank and hearty, that I did not scruple to go; and by degrees the intimacy increased, after some coyness on my part, until, and very shortly, I regularly availed myself of the kindness proffered, whenever not otherwise engaged; and in process of time was rewarded by being told I was "*digne d'être Français!*" the highest compliment that a foreigner can receive in Paris.

I occasionally met there officers of high standing in the French army; but the family lived very quietly, the only guest besides myself being a sort of *aide-de-camp*, whose chief duty seemed that of escorting *Madame* in her drives or promenades on the *Boulevards*. After coffee, the carriage was in waiting for a drive to the Bois de Boulogne, or elsewhere, generally followed by taking an ice at Tortoni's, and a stroll along the Boulevard des Italiens, a part always quite thronged between eight and nine o'clock; the evening occasionally ended by driving to the Champs Elysées to hear *les trompettes Anglaises*, a light brigade being encamped just at the entrance to them. The 52nd Regiment had some good performers on the key-bugle (an instrument unknown to the French), who always played for some time at tattoo, and had usually a crowd of admirers.

An interesting sight, which I witnessed, was the descent of the four Venetian horses from the triumphal arch in the Place Carrousel At the request of the Austrian Emperor, who said he had no officer present who would undertake their removal, the Duke of Wellington committed the task to Major Todd, an able officer of the Royal Staff Corps, whose fertility in expedients under difficulties had been on several occasions evinced in the Peninsula. As the horses stood in view of the King's windows at the Tuileries, it was settled, from a feeling of delicacy, that the work necessary should be performed during the hours of darkness. Accordingly. Todd began his preparations at nightfall, with a few officers, and a score of workmen of his own corps, furnished with hammers and chisels to loosen the horses, which were fixed upon the arch by means of lead.

The first operation was proceeding briskly, when suddenly a clattering of arms was heard in the narrow staircase of the arch, and a number of armed men belonging to the National Guard emerged, and, for the first time within the memory of man, a British position was carried at the point of the bayonet.

When Todd and his people were driven down as prisoners, a mob had collected, and a tumult arose; but with the city occupied by the allied troops, it was not likely that any serious consequences would result. Still, it was not pleasant to be driven along with bayonets in close proximity to their persons. In this manner they were thrust within the precincts of the Tuileries, up to the main entrance of the palace, and, ascending a flight of steps, entered the hall, while the mob was thrust back by the King's Guard.

Although I have made no mention of myself, I was unluckily involved in this scrape, for, as I had heard of the intended removal of the horses, curiosity prompted me to go and see the *modus operandi*, and so I became a prisoner with the rest, my asseveration that I was on the arch merely as a spectator being of no avail, for I met with nothing but a volley of *sacrés*, and the point of a bayonet, which I actually felt on my person.

Shortly after we had entered the hall, the King's first minister, the Duc de Richelieu, came downstairs, and politely inquired how we came to be there; and I, at Todd's request, and happening to be the best Frenchman of the party, explained what had occurred. The Duke was, or pretended to be, in entire ignorance of the intention to remove the horses, and suggested that after the interruption of the work, it would be advisable to attempt nothing more that evening, and he would see into the matter. But how were we to make good our retreat, with an excited mob waiting outside? The Duke whispered to an officer, who then led us through the palace to the front entrance, and, passing into the gardens, we gained the Rue de Rivoli. Todd went straight to Wellington, to make his report, which made His Grace very wroth, who vowed that he would spare the King's feelings no longer. He at once applied to the Emperor of Austria for a sufficient guard to protect the officers and workmen on the following day, resolving that the work should be executed by daylight.

Determined to see the result, I went next morning to the Place Carrousel, and found the square lined by a body of 3000 Austrian troops, composed of infantry, cavalry, and artillery, which force was maintained till the business was concluded, a couple of days later. I witnessed the descent of the famed horses, the Carrousel presenting at the time an imposing spectacle. Along three sides of the square, ranged two deep, was a splendid body of Austrian *cuirassiers*, in white uniform and black helmets, in front of whom stood 2000 of the Hungarian Guards, composed of the finest men I ever saw under arms, also dressed in white, the whole being flanked by artillery, with lighted match, ready for instant action, had madness prompted the mob to offer interruption to the work in hand. As each horse was safely lowered, acclamations arose from the troops, mingled with groans from the populace, who thronged in the rear, and out of sight. Todd was rewarded by the thanks of the Emperor Francis, together with a gold snuff-box, in testimony of the able manner in which his task was executed. It was indeed cleverly done.

The front of the car to which the horses were attached was ornamented by a gilded spread-eagle of large size, which—shall I avow an intended larceny?—I planned to carry off, and for that purpose engaged a couple of the workmen to loosen the screws which held it to the car, and on leaving work the same men were to bag the bird, and convey it to my quarters, It happened, however, that some Prussian officers chanced to mount upon the arch while the workmen were away at dinner-time, when, finding the Imperial bird ready to take wing, their organs of acquisitiveness—for a development of which, by the way, our Prussian friends were celebrated—could not resist the tempting bird, which somehow disappeared, but how, and unobserved, I could not imagine, as the figure was very large; probably it now adorns some military institution at Berlin, instead of the United Service Museum in Scotland Yard.

CHAPTER 11

To England

While in Paris, my military duties being light, I had ample time to enjoy the pleasures that meretricious capital afforded, and passed nearly four months very agreeably.

One morning, as I was about to start upon a party of pleasure, an orderly dragoon appeared, and handed me an official-looking packet, the contents of which rather startled me. The first letter I opened was from the Quartermaster-General, Sir George Murray, to inform me that the Duke of Wellington had no objection to my accepting Sir Hudson Lowe's offer if it suited my views. The next was from Sir Hudson to me, saying he had been appointed to the Government of St Helena, and the "Horse Guards" having agreed to his desire for a detachment of the Royal Staff Corps to go thither, he had expressed a wish for me to accompany it.

Now this was all very flattering, and I at once resolved to accept the proposal.

I think I had reason to feel surprised, as well as flattered, a mere boy of twenty, to be chosen by a man of Sir Hudson's experience to accompany him on his important duty; for although, whilst serving under him in Belgium, he had shown me marks of kindness, and even more than once placed trust in my discretion, still, I was by no means prepared to imagine that I could have any place in his thoughts. It is true that I ever served him to the best of my ability, but it was in a very subordinate capacity. I always looked up to him as to a superior man, who seemed to have no other thoughts but scrupulously to perform his duties, and see that those around him performed theirs.

We liked him much, and were sorry when he left us. I can remember his attending the Duke in an examination of much of the ground between Brussels and the frontier, and his suggesting the propriety of raising some fieldworks, precisely where our great battle was fought.[1] I believe I have stated that he left us for an independent command in the Mediterranean.[2]

It chanced that Colonel the Hon. Dawson Darner was to leave Paris in a day or two with the Duke's despatches, which would frank his journey, and my excellent friend Colonel Torrens having told him that I was also bound for England, he kindly offered me a seat in his carriage, by which I was enabled to perform the journey free of cost.

This arrangement rather hurried me, for I had horses and sundries to dispose of, and various matters to arrange, friends to take leave of, etc. I parted with regret from the family of Monsieur Marchand, who had, during the whole of my stay, quite overwhelmed me with attentions; indeed, I seldom dined away from their table. By that time, Colonel Nicolay had been joined by his very pretty, sprightly, and clever wife (now, while I write in March 1877, Lady Nicolay is still alive, and in the enjoyment of her faculties, at the age of 91!). To both I was under great obligations. My little *factotum* I had to send by way of Ostend, to pick up part of my baggage in depot there.

It was only on the eve of my departure I became aware of a passport being necessary; I immediately hastened to our Ambassador's to obtain one, but was too late, his Secretary having left the office. Here was an awkward dilemma; Colonel Dawson had arranged to start next morning, and without a passport I could not travel. It has been said that necessity is the mother of invention, and so I found it on this occasion. I went off to the office of the quarter-master-general to ask for a military route; but again had the disappointment of finding no officer present, only a clerk in charge, to whom I was well known.

Having obtained a sheet of foolscap paper, I sat down and penned a most formal and imposing document, wherein all authorities, civil and military, were requested, not only to let me pass freely to Calais, but also to afford me aid and protection in case of need. It was written in French, all in due form; then, as no official document is valid abroad without an official seal, I obtained the office one, as large as a

---

1. Sir Hudson Lowe had written as follows: "Should any intermediate post be taken up between the frontiers and Brussels, supposing the latter line of operation be thought the most suitable—*query* in respect to the construction of a work it Mont St Jean at the junction of two principal *chaussées*.
2. In June 1815 Sir Hudson Lowe left the Low Countries to take up the command of the British troops at Genoa, which were to act with the Austro-Sardinian army and the fleet under Lord Exmouth on the southern coast of France.

crown piece, and my *feuille de route* only wanted signing. This, however, caused no difficulty, for I appended my own name, but so written and adorned with flourishes that no Frenchman could possibly decipher it. My passport was demanded two or three times on our way, and found to be quite *en règle*. Of course Sir George Murray did not become aware of this little matter, as I did not tell the clerk about it; but it was in truth a pardonable bit of trickery, such as the circumstances of my case warranted.

On halting at Boulogne to take some refreshment, the waiter suggested that we might perhaps be spared the journey to Calais by taking a passage in a fishing vessel, which could land us at Dover. On inquiring, we found that a Boulogne lugger was about to start, and would take us to Dover for four *napoleons*; so we agreed upon the matter. Considering the state of feeling in France after the battle of Waterloo, it was perhaps not altogether prudent in English officers to entrust themselves to the crew of a fishing boat, and, indeed, it was not reassuring when the skipper, or head man, observing a brace of pistols in my possession, took them, saying he would put them in a safe place. However, we reached Dover after a rapid passage, that is, got within a few hundred yards of the pier, when a boat came off to take us on shore, for which we had to pay two guineas. Precious sharks are, or were, the Dover men!

It is beyond my province to venture any criticism of the Waterloo campaign, but as my scribblings are not for the public, I shall append one or two remarks, the result, in after years, of a careful study of it I know it is a sort of treason to cast blame on the great Duke, but, as was said by Napoleon, "*Qui n'a pas fait des fautes n'a pas fait la guerre.*"

"*All's well that ends well;*" but I think it likely that an impartial and competent critic might find much to criticise in the brief Waterloo campaign, both on the part of the French and of the Allies. Without assuming that I am myself warranted in casting blame on commanders like Napoleon, Wellington, and Blücher, I may perhaps, as having studied carefully all the operations of the campaign, be allowed to hazard a few remarks, which may be taken, as the saying is, for what they are worth.

First, as both Blücher and Wellington had every reason to expect that Napoleon would open the ball, ought they not to have had their armies more in hand, and nearer each other? Wellington's army had been cantoned in the eastern portion of Belgium, by divisions, for several weeks, continuing in the same cantonments up to the opening of hostilities. In this respect the Prussians were not so much disseminated, and were therefore more rapidly collected. Then, as the two armies were destined to co-operate, why was there so great a gap left between them—some forty miles—and this, when expecting the onset of the greatest and most energetic captain of modern times? The tardiness of the allied generals, especially Wellington, may be said to have jeopardised! the fate of Europe; forbad both armies been so situated as to afford each other mutual support, a single battle would have settled the campaign; for the Allies would have engaged with a force nearly double that of the French; the result, therefore, could scarcely have been doubtful. Whereas, by the faulty disposition of the Allies, previous to the commencement of hostilities, Napoleon gained the immense advantage of fighting them In succession, beating Blücher, and going very near to beating Wellington.

Had Ney acted with more vigour in assailing our position at Quatre Bras, and gained possession of that important point, the communication between Wellington and Blücher would have been completely cut off, and been attended with the worst consequences.

The Duke had taken it into his head that his right might be turned by way of Hal; but surely such a manoeuvre could never have been imagined by Napoleon, for, had our right been turned, it would only have forced us towards the Prussians. But this notion of the Duke paralysed two divisions that were left near Hal, when their presence was much needed at Waterloo. But nothing succeeds like success. The Duke is reported to have said that, if he got into a scrape, his soldiers got him out of it. I cannot but think that Waterloo was a striking instance.

Napoleon at St. Helena

CHAPTER 12

Aboard the 'Phaeton'

My detachment of the Royal Staff Corps, consisting of a sergeant and sixteen men, had been hurried from Hythe to Hilsea Barracks (near Portsmouth), for *immediate* embarkation, late in October 1815, where I joined it, and obtained a lodging at Kingston Cross, about a mile on the road to Portsmouth; the frigate *Phaeton*, however, which was to take a new Governor and suite to St Helena, and on board of which I and my men were to sail, only arrived at Spithead towards the end of December, when I got an order to embark.

Having to wait some time on the wharf, my sergeant begged me to advance money to enable the men to lay in a few necessaries, a request which I, most unwisely, acceded to—the consequence being that many of them, like true British soldiers, got drunk. When all had staggered in, the boat started and we gained the ship, but some of the men, being unable to climb up the side, had to be hoisted on board, to my infinite mortification.

Next day the Governor, his family, and officers came off, and to-wards evening the anchor was raised, and we sailed.[1] Scarcely had we cleared the Isle of Wight, when the wind rose, and the sky looked threatening. Before the topsails could be reefed, the gale was upon us. My cot was slung in the "steerage" amongst the *middies*, a confined and wretched place in the olden time; but repose that night was out of the question, for, the gale having come so suddenly, there had been no time to get boxes, etc., fixed, so that they were knocked to and fro as the ship lurched and pitched, causing indescribable noise and confusion; the hubbub on deck, too, was alone enough to prevent sleep. In short, I felt as if in Pandemonium, and longed for day.

---

1. The *Phaeton* sailed 29th January 1816.

The deck next morning was strewed with *débris*; there lay the main-topsail yard broken in two pieces, with other damaged spars; sails in tatters amid a confusion of ropes were scattered about. Through the exertions of our energetic first lieutenant, in the course of the short December day. the chaos was restored to order, in spite of the heavy gale which continued.

Nothing ever made a greater impression upon me than the grandeur of the warring elements above, and the magnificence of the tremendous sea when crossing the Bay of Biscay. How I enjoyed sitting on the taffrail, watching the noble vessel plunging head foremost into its depths, as if going to the bottom, and then rising majestically, as having only made her *salaam* to vast and threatening power!

We had the same weather all the way to Madeira, where we anchored. I went on shore with one of the lieutenants, named Hoare, who, having purchased a quarter-cask of wine, left me to go and get some provisions for the gun-room mess. When we met again, he was issuing from a store, and on my asking whether he had obtained what he wanted, he said yes, but that he had been dealing with a rascal. The shopkeeper heard and understood the meaning of the last word. looked viciously, and seemed about to strike. Hoare seized a ham in self-defence, and as the man was trying to rescue it, it fell into a barrel of flour, and as my companion was about to withdraw from the affray, his opponent flung the ham at him, and covered him with flour. This ended the fight, not greatly to the credit of the naval uniform, I fear. Having cleaned his coat and epaulette, we adjourned to the hotel, where, as one of the officers of the frigate told us, "One could not open one's mouth under a dollar, nor shut it under two."

Hoare had sent off his wine to be put on board, but was annoyed to find, on regaining the frigate, that the captain had refused to allow it to be received, and had ordered it back to the shore. This was most annoying to Hoare, who represented the serious inconvenience it would cause; but the captain was obdurate, although Hoare said the cask could be put into his own cabin. Shortly after, it was Hoare's turn to dine with the captain; this he declined to do, and for such a breach of naval etiquette and discipline, he was placed in close arrest, and so remained during several weeks, until Sir Hudson Lowe made intercession on his behalf.

In these steaming days, when mail ships make the run from Plymouth to St Helena within a fortnight, the reader will learn with surprise that our fast sailing frigate was three months on her voyage.

Regardless of winds, a steamer goes direct to her destination, whereas the trade winds, which in the Atlantic are constant within the tropics, blowing towards the equator from the north-east and south-east, compel a sailing vessel to cross the ocean, till almost reaching South America, when she in able to alter her course, and make, to use a seaman's term, southing, until, having got out of the south-east trade wind, and into the "variables," she can make "easting."

Such was the course formerly commonly pursued. I say commonly, for what is tamed the eastern passage, namely, by hugging the African coast, and so making a more direct course, was seldom taken by ships for the Cape of Good Hope and India; the objection being that lengthened calms often render the progress very uncertain. It was adopted, however, by Admiral Sir George Cockburn and his squadron, when carrying out Napoleon, and performed in ten weeks.

The voyage of the *Phaeton* was unmarked by any incident, save that of failing in with a ship in about the latitude of the Cape of Good Hope, which looking very suspicious, our captain sent an officer to ascertain her quality. She proved, as was suspected, a slave ship, having on board three hundred Africans, but could not be interfered with, since her papers showed, or pretended to show, that she was only taking the slaves from one Portuguese settlement to another, which was then permitted by law.

Our good ship continued to be steered as if for the Cape, when, being far enough to the east, she turned towards St Helena, and getting into the south-east trade wind, was carried to the island in ten or twelve days more.

Knowing nothing of navigation, and as we had seen no land since leaving Madeira, I felt admiration for the precision with which we dropped down upon the diminutive island. For several days the officers on whom the navigation depended had been unusually busy with their sextants and chronometers, and hopes were expressed that we should not miss the isle, as had done the *Glatton* 64, acquiring thereby the unenviable name of "blind *Glatton*"—a mishap which sometimes befell ships, and was indeed experienced by two fine frigates a few weeks after our arrival, bearing Admiral Sir Pulteney Malcolm and three foreign commissioners. We saw them one morning a long way to leeward, and it took them an entire day to "beat up "to the anchorage.

Surely the heart of Napoleon must have sunk within him at sight of the forbidding aspect of the dark lofty mass the island presents;

for its windward side looks like a gigantic perpendicular ragged wall, some fifteen hundred or two thousand feet high, showing apparently not a fissure by which it could be entered. But on the leeward side are several ravines, inviting you, as It were, to scramble up them and gain the interior.

As the trade wind does not vary in its direction, the island serves as a huge breakwater, under the shelter of which vessels can anchor anywhere along the shore where there is "holding" ground. But as a rule they lie opposite the town, for obvious reasons.

On rounding the eastern part of the island, we came in sight of the flag-ship at her anchorage, and fired the usual salute to the flag, which was duly returned. Meanwhile, our cable had been prepared for anchoring, but, by some untoward accident or negligence, the anchor slipped, dragging after it the cable. There was nothing for it but to let It run out, or the frigate would have been arrested in her course a mile or two short of the anchorage, which would have been awkward indeed.

The aspect of the pretty little town from the anchorage is very inviting, with its neat little church, its white houses of an English type, and ornamented by a sprinkling of cocoa-nut trees on the left hand, rising from the botanical garden. The valley or ravine is just wide enough for the buildings, the bills, or rather mountains, rising on each hand to a height of about six hundred feet, where they overlook the sea, but gradually becoming higher, till they attain an elevation of from twelve hundred to fifteen hundred feet. They are not generally precipitous, the slopes not much exceeding 50° and presenting alternately ledges of rock and indurated clay.

On landing, we military officers went to the boarding-house of Mr Saul Solomon, and were well entertained at a cost of thirty shillings *per diem* each, and fifteen shillings per servant, I remained there but four days, for which six pounds seemed to me an extravagance for a subaltern officer. In conjunction with Lieutenant Wortham, of the Royal Engineers, a lodging was hired, and we shook the dust off our feet at the door of Mr Solomon.

At a part called Deadwood, six miles from the town, some wooden barracks recently from England were in process of erection. and my men were wanted for the work. To enable me to visit them, the Governor kindly lent me a horse from his stables for this purpose.

Two roads lead from the town to the upper regions, one towards the eastern, the other to the western part of the island. These have

View of Jamestown

been practised in the sides of the mountains zigzag fashion. My duty carried me in the eastern direction. To reach Deadwood I had to pass the entrance to Longwood, which I longed to explore, and to fall in with some of the French persons there; but without special permission, no one, whether military or civil, could pass in. At length my curiosity was partially gratified, when, riding with Sir George Bingham, a gallant soldier in command of the troops, who won his K.CB. by good service in the Peninsula under Wellington, he proposed a visit to the Countess Bertrand, then residing in a small house about a mile short of Longwood. I found Madame Bertrand very agreeable and chatty. She questioned me about Paris, with all the yearning of a Frenchwoman for that *abode of bliss* [2] She was very tall and graceful, though not a beauty. Soon after I had opportunities of seeing her often, and we became very good friends.

Her husband we met on remounting our horses, and I was presented to him. He wore a military dress, which was truly French from far above the crown of his head to his feet; for his cocked-hat was of the loftiest, while his legs were encased in jack-boots reaching to mid thigh. A blue coat, thrown open so as to show an expanse of white waistcoat, across which was displayed the blue riband of the Legion of Honour, and nankeen small clothes completed the dress of General Count Bertrand. He seemed a man on the wrong side of fifty, perhaps he was fifty-five; [3] his hair, like Marmion's, was "*coal black and grizzled here and there;*" he wore a melancholy, depressed look, shrugged his shoulders like most of his countrymen, and his demeanour was quiet and impressive.

My first entry to Longwood was with the Governor, when, meeting the Count de Montholon, I was presented to him. The count was a sort of *maire du palais*, and ruled the household. In introducing me, the Governor said that I should be almost daily there, and if any repairs were wanted, he was to apply to me. After this, I saw him from time to time, on little business matters, but it was long before we became really acquainted. Indeed, from not feeling drawn towards him, I was so remiss as not to pay my respects to his countess; but we became very good friends in time, as will be seen.

The count was rather short, standing under five feet seven inches;

2. Madame Bertrand was a Creole. Her father, General Arthur Dillon, was an Irishman in the French service who perished in the Revolution.
3. General Bertrand was forty-two at this time, and Count de Montholon thirty-two.

he never wore a military dress, but always appeared in jack-boots like Bertrand. His age about forty, and he was good-looking, with dark complexion.

Count Las Cases and General Gourgaud I first met at the house of Mr Balcombe—The Briars—where Napoleon had been accommodated for many weeks, while Longwood House was being prepared for his reception—occupying a kind of summer-house detached from the main dwelling. On introducing me to Las Cases, our host gave him a merciless slap on the back, saying, "This is my friend Las Cases." As may be imagined, the poor little man winced under so unusual a style of introduction, but soon recovered from the shock. He had been an emigrant in England for several years, and spoke our language with facility.

A dwelling for Count Bertrand being under construction near Longwood House, and the shell nearly completed, I had to see the rest of the work carried on, and the Governor desired me to attend to the Countess's wishes as far as possible. She lost no time in availing herself of my delegated authority by proposing to have a verandah added. Thinking this to be somewhat more than the Governor contemplated in his orders to me. I consulted him about it "By all means," he said, "have a verandah erected."

Then I consulted the lady as to its dimensions. "You must make it wide," she said, "as it will serve for the children to play in." Well, from one thing to another, the verandah became a good-sized room, and I used to compliment the Countess on her cleverness in verandah planning.

When superintending this addition to the house, I saw that lady constantly, and we became pretty intimate, but her husband was not often visible, being much in attendance upon his master; however, I learned to like him, respecting him too for his fidelity to Napoleon, and thinking him a sensible, discreet man, but not possessing remarkable ability; and longer acquaintance served to satisfy me that my early impressions were not incorrect.

With General Gourgaud I soon was on friendly terms, and paid him frequent visits, which seemed to afford him pleasure in his rather solitary situation; for, save with the Bertrands, he had no social intercourse with any, though living under the same roof as the Montholons and Las Cases. I say under the same roof, seeing that a large addition had been made to Longwood House, all one storey high, in order to lodge the Montholons, Las Cases, Gourgaud, the surgeon O'Meara, and a Captain of the Line, as general observer of all that went on in connection with the establishment, but especially to make sure that Napoleon was safe, but which, indeed, he had scant means of ascertaining.

The Briars, Napoleon's first residence at St. Helena

CHAPTER 13

St. Helena

Notwithstanding my daily presence at Longwood, and often strolling round the house and in the garden, I saw nothing of our great captive for several months, all my watchings for a glimpse of him proving vain. At length, when riding one day close to the house, on turning a corner, I came plump upon three figures advancing, the centre person wearing his small cocked-hat square to the front, the others, one walking on each side of Napoleon, bareheaded. Turning a little aside to get out of the way, I took off my hat and made a low bow, which was returned by Napoleon raising his. He was dressed just as we see him in his portraits, *viz.*, with a green cut-away military coat, white waistcoat, breeches, and silk stockings; of course he bore the tri-coloured cockade, and the star of the Legion of Honour.

Occasionally, but very rarely, I have seen him strolling in the garden, when, of course, I took care to avoid, if possible, his seeing me. Keeping himself, as he did, much secluded, in fact seldom leaving the house for weeks together, the orderly captain on duty, whose business it was to ascertain one way or another that the captive was safe, had an arduous and unsatisfactory task to perform.

Shortly after the arrival of the Governor at the island, Sir George Cockburn carried him round the island in his flag-ship, the *Northumberland* 74; a trip in which he was accompanied by several officers, including myself. We were on board a couple of days, and landed at two or three places when practicable; but only once on the windward side, at a little inlet called Sandy Bay, which is in some degree sheltered from the surf, and where boats can enter unless the wind is very strong, and consequently the surf great Coming to a part where a huge rock stands separated from the island by a narrow passage, the Admiral, after speaking to the sailing-master, ordered the ship to be steered through it, which would have been hazardous, save for the steady trade wind, which was favourable, and precluded all danger.

When the ship came abreast of a part called "Holdfast-Tom," where, according to tradition, our sailors. when they captured the island, effected a landing and scaled the precipice, some fifteen hundred feet high, the Governor called me to him, and said, "You are an active young fellow; what say you to being landed, and mounting the rocks up to a point where a picket of soldiers is stationed?" This being just before the dinner hour, my appetite prompted me with an amendment, *viz.*, that I should on some future occasion attempt to descend, instead of mount, the apparently inaccessible crags.

Although not much given to joking, I think it likely His Excellency did not really intend me to make trial of my scaling powers; and I fancied I observed a twinkle in the Admiral's eye, as he said he thought my proposition was perhaps the best. A few days later, I took two of my men, provided with ropes, and the descent was accomplished, though at some risk to our necks, by making our way down an adjacent ravine, if I may so term a division between jagged rocks, and we ended the rather perilous adventure by climbing up the precipitous rocks, as the sailors are said to have done, to the no small surprise of the picket, the corporal of which informed me that the men were in the habit of getting down to the shore by what he called a path for the purpose of fishing.

This reminds me of a sad catastrophe which befell two officers of the 66th Regiment, who, having got down by the corporal's path, were fishing from the extremity of a ledge of rocks, jutting some distance into the sea, when one of those "rollers," occasionally witnessed in the Atlantic, coming suddenly upon them, both were swept into eternity. A soldier attending upon them, who at the moment was engaged in seeking small crabs as bait, nearer the shore, happily escaped.

As the *Northumberland* kept quite close to the land, especially when on the windward side, our trip was highly interesting; stupendous perpendicular rocks, at a height of two thousand feet, in certain parts, seeming to dwarf the line-of-battle ship to a mere cock-boat—at least such she must have appeared to an observer on the summit; all was truly sublime, but far from beautiful, as not a vestige of vegetation could be seen.

I have more than once spoken of the rugged and bare appearance of the island as viewed from without, but have said little of its interior. The forbidding shell has, however, a kernel of a totally different character, being diversified by hill and dale and refreshing verdure; not only in the bottoms of the valleys, but also on the hill slopes there is grass, but a dearth of trees throughout, save at Longwood, where the monotonous gum-wood covers an area of thirty or forty acres.

We found tolerable bridle-roads, zigzagging up and down the hills, but only two real highways, such as wheels could roll on; one, as before mentioned, leading to Longwood from the town, the other to Plantation House, the country residence of the Governor; but at the period I am scribbling about, the only carriage ever seen was a very ancient one, drawn by four bullocks, which at rare intervals carried Lady Lowe between the Governor's town and country houses; and also such of her fair visitors as were judged worthy the honour of travelling at a snail's pace in the old vehicle.

This casual mention of Lady Lowe reminds me that I owe an apology to her memory for not sooner introducing her, as she was no ordinary person. Her Ladyship was a sister of my former chief, Sir William Delancey, who fell at Waterloo, a widow somewhat over forty[1] when she married Sir Hudson Lowe, on the eve of his departure for St Helena; she was altogether a very attractive person, being pretty, elegant, possessing a sprightly wit, and great conversational powers, with excellent taste in her toilette. Her presence made the dinner parties of Plantation House very agreeable, and, as the table and wines were of superior quality, our visits thither were truly enjoyable.

Lady Lowe was formed to please in any society, and in after years it was said that the Prince Regent saw her often at the Pavilion, and admired her; nay, the gossips of Brighton went so far as to fancy that Lady C—— became alarmed for her empire, and very *heartily* congratulated Lady Lowe, when Sir Hudson was named for a West India Government; in thanking Lady C——, she made her look rather blank, by saying she had no intention of going with him. Probably all this was just idle gossip, with no foundation.[2]

I shall now attempt a slight sketch of the worthy Governor. He stood five feet seven, spare in make, having good features, fair hair, and eyebrows overhanging his eyes; his look denoted penetration and firmness, his manner rather abrupt, his gait quick, his look and general

1. Lady Lowe was thirty-five at this time.
2. "My mother and Lady C—— never exchanged a word. My mother was never but once at the Pavilion during George IV.'s time, and then it was at a children's Twelfth Night Ball in 1825, when was six years old. The King spoke to us, but Lady C—— never came near us."—Note by Miss Lowe.

demeanour indicative of energy and decision. He wrote or dictated rapidly and was fond of writing, was well read in military history, spoke French and Italian with fluency; was warm and steady in his friendships, and popular, both with the inhabitants of the isle and the troops. His portrait, prefixed to Mr Forsyth's book, is a perfect likeness.

I have said that with Sir Pulteney Malcolm came three foreign commissioners, Russian, French, and Austrian. The first, Count Balmain, was a very plain sample of the Tartar, holding the rank of colonel; was clever, well-informed, and conversable. The Marquis de Montchenu was a perfect representation of the *ancien régime*—a man of nearly seventy, who had been many years an *émigré* in Germany, apparently seeing nothing of that country, nor acquiring a word of its language. Speaking of him on some occasion, with a Frenchman who knew mankind, and French *kind* especially, he observed, "I have always thought Louis XVIII. an able man, but he never showed it more than in sending the Marquis de Montchenu to look after Bonaparte at St Helena." The Austrian, Baron Stürmer, was a true *diplomate* of the Metternich school, polished in manner, quiet and gentlemanly in demeanour, and a man of some ability. Of the trio of commissioners, he was the only one married; his wife was an exceedingly pretty Parisian, but *voilà tout*.

These gentlemen never got access to Napoleon, who would not receive them; they gave the Governor some trouble in seeking to render themselves of consequence; they mixed not in society, and one and all seemed intent on saving money. They were a useless expense to their several Governments, and it may well be asked, *que diable allaient-ils faire dans cette galère?* The Russian and Austrian had a joint *ménage* in a pretty country house about four miles from James Town; the Frenchman lived in the town itself, and, as he liked whist, was always ready to come to our little card meetings, held in turn at the lodgings of a few officers of the like proclivity, where slight refreshments were given; and, as for a very long time we were not asked to meet at his house, one of our wags dubbed him Marquis de *Monter chez nous*—a good play upon Montchenu. *Au reste*, he was pompous and harmless, giving less trouble than the others.

A little brig had sailed from Portsmouth about a month before we started, with a cargo of nine horses, belonging to the Governor and officers of the staff, and through Sir Hudson's kind intervention I was permitted to embark one that I picked up at Portsmouth; but week after week passed, and still no brig made its appearance. Concluding at length that the little craft must have gone either to Otaheite or to the bottom, I was agreeably surprised to learn that a very small brig was in sight, which turned out to be our horse transport. Probably her captain knew no more of navigation than what enabled him to reach London from Newcastle, and hence it is not surprising that he had spent between five and six months groping about the ocean, peeping in at Brazil and other places. Marvellous to say, only two of the animals died during an incarceration of so many months in the vessel's hold, never lying down, nor having exercise save what the pitching and rolling of the brig gave them.

But I must bear in mind that all real interest connected with the island is centred at Longwood, and that the treatment of the great captive by our Governor is a matter of importance, especially as regards the reputation of the latter, which I trust these pages may help to place in its proper light.

When chatting one day with Count Bertrand, I expressed regret that, as a mere subaltern. I had little chance of being presented to Napoleon. To my great surprise, he said that possibly it might be managed, and he would think of it Not long afterwards, recurring to the subject, he said that Napoleon was not indisposed to receive me, and, if I would bring Major Emmett, he thought he could contrive to have us both presented. Now Emmett (our Commanding Royal Engineer) was known to entertain very liberal sentiments in politics, and hence was in some favour at Longwood; doubtless, the idea of receiving me arose from a desire of Bonaparte to have a talk with him. On telling Emmett what Bertrand had let fall, he was much pleased, and agreed to accompany me to Longwood.

We went thither accordingly, and, on calling at Count Bertrand's house, were told by the countess that her husband was with Napoleon; after waiting as long as politeness allowed, in expectation of the count's appearing, we took our leave, and were about to go away *re infectâ* when we encountered Mr O'Meara, and, on telling him our object, he said he thought he could assist us. He went at once to Napoleon's apartments, and returned in a few minutes to say that Napoleon would see us presently; Bertrand then came out, and desired us to follow him.

On entering the drawing-room, we found Napoleon standing at the fireplace, leaning on the mantelshelf, with cocked-hat in hand, evidently a studied position. When we were announced he advanced towards us, and, addressing my companion, the following dialogue took place. (I shall give Bonaparte's questions in French *verbatim*, as I noted them down on the same evening.)

"*Combien avez-vous de service?*"

"Nine years."

"*Où avez-vous servi?*"

"In Spain, Portugal, France, and America."

"*Vous avez fait des sièges?*"

"Yes, those of Ciudad Rodrigo and Badajos."

"*Vous avez manqué la brèche ài Badajos, un peu brusqué la chose?*"

"We were obliged to risk an assault, and had it failed, we must have raised the siege. It would then have been doubtful whether, with our scanty means, the place could have been taken."

"*Eh! cependant les places se prennent. Vous aviez du canon à Elvas—de combien est Elvas éloigné de Badajos?*"

"Three leagues."

"*Ah! trios lieues; ce seraient donc les projectiles et le transport qui auraient causé des difficultés; mais la Guadiana est navigable, n'est-ce pas? Non, ah! Que faisiez-vous donc de votre argent? Quand il n'y a pas d'autres moyens de se rendre maître d'une place, il faut ouvrir la bourse et farmer les yeux.*"

Napoleon then spoke of Burgos, when Emmett said that a horn-work there had created a difficulty, upon which Napoleon, with animation, said that he had ordered its construction.

"*Est-ce qu'il fut emporté?*"

"Yes, on the first night."

"*D'assaut?*"

"Yes, by assault."

"*Il n'était donc pas défendu?*"

"It was defended, but was entered by the gorge."

"*Est-ce que la gorge n'était pas palissadée?*"

"The palissades were cut down."

Napoleon then referred to the celebrated lines of Torres Vedras, seeming to think that Masséna ought to have attacked them.

Lastly, Napoleon, alluding to two or three block-houses then in course of erection at the island, asked what Emmett expected to attack them, "*est-ce les rats et les souris?*" We were then dismissed.

During the interview, I was standing very close to the great man, observing him narrowly. I estimated his height at something under five feet seven. His make thick about the shoulders, with very short neck; eyes grey, which at times appeared wholly devoid of expression. He was habited as I have already described him.

In process of time, Count de Montholon threw off his reserve towards me, and our acquaintance grew into intimacy. He told me that he was constantly engaged in writing to dictation, and, that frequently he was sent for in the night-time, when Napoleon could not sleep, and so employed for many hours. One morning I met him with a quantity of foolscap writing paper in his hand, which he allowed me to glance at; it had evidently been hastily scrawled over in pencil. "Now," he said, "I must set to work to transcribe and curtail all this, to be ready for inspection when called for."

If what follows may be relied on, it would seem that the great man and his scribe were not always of one mind in their work. Meeting Montholon again, armed with his roll of foolscap, and asking how the memoirs were proceeding, his reply was that he had just quarrelled with the Emperor, who would insist that prosody signified the art of versifying.

"We were speaking of Rogniat,[3] who says that war can be reduced to certain principles, and that he who is master of those principles *connaît la guerre*; the Emperor observed that this assertion was a *grande bêtise*, that, although the study of tactics teaches how to manoeuvre troops, it requires genius to become a great captain, which assuredly cannot be acquired by study; and that Rogniat might as well have said that the study of *solfège* teaches how to compose *chefs-d'œuvres* of music, and that of prosody to become a poet like Homer or Virgil.

"I," said Montholon, "ventured to remark that it was *poétique* he meant, and not prosody, which has quite another signification. He replied, No; that *poétique* sounds poor, insipid, *ne frappe pas l'oreille*, whereas *prosodie, prosopopée, cela frappe l'oreille*.' I took the liberty to observe that neither *prosodie* nor *prosopopée* taught the art of making verses. 'Say then rhetoric,' was the rejoinder.

"'Neither does rhetoric,' I replied. Then the Emperor became angry, telling me I so altered his dictation *qu'il ne s'y reconnaissait pas*, completely spoiling his style, which all the world allowed to be original. 'But, Sire,' I said, 'where can we find your style? I am not acquainted with it. May I be so bold as to ask what you have written to show it?'

"'Look,' he said, 'at my proclamations, my articles in the *Moniteur*.'

"'But, Sire, I do not perceive in those any marks of style; you blunt-

3. General Rogniat, of the French Engineers, had just published a, Treatise on War.

LONGWOOD

ly express your ideas, and that is all; and as regards articles of greater length which have appeared as your own, I do not know of any two which resemble each other in style. Can you say that your *discours au Champ de Mai, et le Manifeste contre la Maison d'Autricke sont de la même plume?* No, Sire, those who wrote to your dictation retrenched, as I do, all that is superfluous.' Certainly nothing less resembles the true style, or manner, of the Emperor, than that which is attributed to him. The Emperor ended the scene, in great irritation, by vowing he would never dictate another page; to which I replied, that such a resolve was perhaps unfortunate for the world, but that to me it would only be a boon."

The anger of Napoleon soon, however, blew over, and Montholon continued to write and *retrench.* His labours comprised several volumes, which were published in after years, and commanded a certain amount of interest, though less than might have been expected. They are entitled, *Mémoires pour servir à l'Histoire de France*, and, as I think, do credit to Montholon's pen and judgement.

I presume that no one will doubt that Napoleon had an intense hatred of England, and of everything English; but, if he gave utterance to remarks such as the following, we may infer that his hatred was mingled with profound respect

Meeting Montholon on the day when intelligence came of the sad end of that eminent man Sir Samuel Romilly, he told me he had just left Napoleon, whose remarks upon the occurrence were very striking. According to Montholon, he thus expressed himself: "What a nation are the English! This suicide is as if I had killed myself after Marengo, on learning the death of Josephine. Ah! had I commanded a British army, I might have lost ten battles of Waterloo, without being abandoned by a man from its ranks, or losing a vote in Parliament." Not very complimentary to the French, whether civil or military! But indeed I gathered during my intercourse with the persons at Longwood, that, on the whole, Napoleon entertained anything but a flattering opinion of the nation whose destinies he had so long and so successfully swayed.

I learned with regret in after years, that truthfulness was not the characteristic of Napoleon's adherents at St Helena, but could never see just reason to doubt that what Montholon told me were Napoleon's remarks about the British people and army was really said.

General Gourgaud, whom I often had a chat with, very soon found himself uncomfortable in the seclusion of Longwood, of which he used to complain to me. It was believed that Napoleon early took a dislike to him; but from whatever cause, I clearly saw that he would gladly leave the island. Count Las Cases had already left, having been detected in violating the established rules by entrusting to a servant of his, who was quitting his service, a letter addressed to a lady in England, containing a communication intended for Lucien Bonaparte, who was residing at Rome. In consequence of this, he and his son, a lad of fourteen, were withdrawn from Longwood, and soon afterwards sent to the Cape of Good Hope.[4]

I do not think that Las Cases and Gourgaud were intimate, but the departure of the former added to the seclusion of the poor general, who, being at bitter enmity with Montholon, saw only the Bertrands, with whom he continued on friendly terms. In such a state of things he naturally got depressed and melancholy, and at length made up his mind to depart. Having communicated his desire to the Governor, the latter was rather embarrassed how to dispose of him, until such time as an opportunity should occur for sending him to the Cape. I was then occupying a couple of rooms in a small cottage, situated in a beautiful part of the island; and Sir Hudson asked me if I could there receive Gourgaud, saying, he proposed it from thinking such an arrangement would be agreeable to him, as we were on very friendly terms. Having but two small rooms at my disposal, this was out of the question; so a house was hired near the Governor's residence, and, at a time appointed, I was deputed to conduct the General thither, and to remain with him.

On our way, we had to pass by Plantation House, and Gourgaud took the opportunity of paying his respects to Sir Hudson, who received us in his library, and, thinking he might like to be *tête-à-tête* with Gourgaud, I left the room. On remounting our horses, the general expressed his great astonishment that the Governor had not sought to take advantage of his excited state to glean from him information about Longwood doings; "*Je ne reviens pas de mon étonnement, non, je n'en reviens pas.*" And certainly the Governor did evince great delicacy, and well might Gourgaud feel astonished.

On that day, and repeatedly afterwards, the general and I dined at Plantation House, and the change from Longwood served to restore his health and spirits. With Lady Lowe he was quite charmed, being able to appreciate her wit and sprightly conversation.

---

4. Las Cases and his son left Longwood 25th November 1816, and St Helena, 30th December.

Plantation House, the residence of Sir Hudson Lowe

I was very pleasantly domiciled with Gourgaud for a couple of months, and having thrown off the *maladie du pays*, he became cheerful. Having been with Napoleon in the fatal expedition to Moscow, he had much to narrate that I found interesting. Most deplorable were his accounts of the disastrous retreat, and of their sufferings from cold and hunger. On one occasion an *aide-de-camp* having got a small quantity of lentils, they furnished quite a feast to a party of the staff.

The house occupied by Baron Stürmer and Count Balmain was within a short walk, and we occasionally visited it, but were never asked either to luncheon or dinner, although great professions were made of desire to show Gourgaud kindness. The baroness was fond of jewellery, and a fine diamond pin worn by the general was much admired. "You must make me a present, as a memorial of our friendship; let it be an *épingle, car ça pique et ça atitche*," was her modest way of evincing her longing desire to possess the diamond; but it proved a failure, as may well be imagined.

Baron Stürmer sent to Prince Metternich an account of conversations held with Gourgaud, which the Prince forwarded to Lord Bathurst. I never could think them worth attention; indeed, the General seemed to enjoy playing upon the curiosity of the two commissioners. Only fancy his asserting that Napoleon could escape from the island at any time! Here is what Stürmer wrote about it:—

Stürmer.—*Pensez-vous qu'il puisse s'échapper d'ici?*

Gourgaud.—*Il en a eu dix fois l'occasion, et il l'a encore au moment même où je vous parle.*

Stürmer.—*Je vous avoue que cela me paraît impossible.*

Gourgaud.—*Eh! que ne fait-on pas quand on a des millions à sa disposition? Au reste, quoique j'aie à me plaindre de l'Empereur, je ne le trahirai jamais. Je le répète, il peut s'évader seul et aller en Amérique quand il le voudra; je n'en dirai pas davantage.*

Stürmer.—*S'il le peut, que ne le fait-il? L'essentiel est d'être hors d'ici.*

Gourgaud.—*Nous le lui avons tous conseillé. Il a toujours combattu nos raisons et y a résisté. Quelque malheureux qu'il soit ici, il jouit secrètement de l'importance qu'on met à sa garde, de l'intérêt qu'y prennent toutes les Puissances de l'Europe, du soin que l'on met à recueillir ses moindres paroles, etc. Il nous a dit plusieurs fois, "je ne peux plus vivre en particulier; j'aime mieux être prisonnier ici que libre aux Etats-Unis."* [5]

Now, while willing enough to tell all he knew about Longwood, Gourgaud gave me little information of any matters of material value. He maintained, however, that there was no difficulty in communicating with England surreptitiously; but this we were aware of, nor could it be prevented, unless all the dwellers at Longwood could have been placed *au secret*. It was found, as we shall see by-and-bye, that Mr O'Meara was the grand medium, as his letters passed freely, that is, they were not subjected to inspection like those written by the French.

At times Gourgaud would talk strangely, even going so far as to more than insinuate that Napoleon had suggested to him self-destruction; this was on an occasion when death by means of the fumes of charcoal was talked of. Of course I believed not a word of this. Then he said that, *à propos* of fame and reputation, Bertrand had declared he would rather be Caesar dead than be himself alive; to which Gourgaud had told him he had only to put a pistol to his head, and so become Caesar or Alexander. In truth, my companion was a foolish, vain fellow, without sense enough to conceal his weaknesses.

Before leaving Longwood, he showed me a sword, on which was depicted a French officer shooting a *cossack* with a pistol, and underneath with a date that I do not remember. *"Le chef de bataillon, Gourgaud, tua un Cosaque qui se précipitait sur l'Empereur."* I may add that Montholon told me this was a myth—at least declared that no such occurrence took place; but which can we believe?

The Governor's instructions required that any of the French who might leave the island, should be sent for a time to the Cape of Good Hope; but, seeing that Gourgaud had been more than two months away from Longwood, and a suitable vessel from India touching at our island on her way home, he very kindly waived his instructions, and engaged a passage in the said vessel; but the poor man was without funds, and what could he do on arrival in England penniless?

In his exigency, Gourgaud resolved to apply to Bertrand, and asked me to go to Longwood and try to obtain a loan. We rode over together, and, leaving the General outside, I found Bertrand at home, engaged with two gentlemen, who proved to be commanders of Indiamen, In the Company's service. Feeling pretty sure of not being understood by those persons, when speaking French, I made my business known. Im-

5. This conversation is given in *Forsyth*, 3,392-394. In the official report of Stürmer's despatches, edited by Dr H. Schlitter, the reader is referred to Forsyth for the report. Dr Schlitter gives only a certain portion of the despatch, omitted by Forsyth.

mediately Bertrand assumed an *unlending* aspect, assuring me, however, that he was quite willing to assist Gourgaud in his difficulty, but that, he having declined to accept a sum offered him by the Emperor, he, Bertrand, could not comply, unless Gourgaud would now consent to receive what had been offered, adding, that it would be disrespectful towards the Emperor were he to accede; his words were, *"qu'il ne me mette pas dans la position de manquer à l'Empereur"*

Whilst the negotiation, if I may so term it, was in progress, the two captains remained seated, Bertrand and I—I was going to say——standing; but, becoming extremely energetic, he closed upon me, repeating again and again the phrase I have italicised, until he pushed me into a corner, whence I could retreat no farther. The scene must have seemed most extraordinary to the two spectators, and I must have been to them an object of commiseration.

On rejoining Gourgaud, and making known my failure, he felt greatly disappointed, having been confident of Bert rand's assistance—vowing, however, that he would not have Napoleon's money—I think 8000 *francs*—for which sum a draft would have been given upon the banker Lafitte, of Paris, who had been entrusted with a large sum by the ex-Emperor.

Of course I immediately informed the Governor of my mission and its results, and on the following morning he enclosed to me a cheque on his own banker for £100, which I handed to Gourgaud, who expressed himself as very grateful On the afternoon of the same day I accompanied him to James Town, to see him safely on board.

It was sunset when we pushed off from the wharf, and, as there is no twilight in the tropics, it was getting dark. We had not got far from the shore, when the guard-boat of the flag-ship stopped us, and the *parole* was demanded. Not expecting to be so late, I had not thought of providing myself with the password, so I explained to the officer in command of the boat the nature of the duty I was upon, but all in vain, so I had only to return and obtain the necessary word. Again we started, only to be again stopped, and peremptorily ordered back although giving the parole, the officer saying his orders were not to allow any boat to approach a vessel after sunset without special permission.

Here was an unfortunate dilemma. The ship had cleared out and was ready to sail; she would not lose precious hours by waiting for a passenger, even though he was a *ci-devant* French general. It then occurred to me to request that we should be taken to the flag-ship, and have the business submitted to her captain. This was assented to, and on explaining the matter to him, he, as the chief authority afloat, ordered the officer in charge of the guard-boat to escort us to the vessel, when I took leave of my charge, and returned to the landing steps, but still escorted by the guard-boat. Gourgaud had thus an opportunity of seeing that leaving the island was attended with no little difficulty. The Governor smiled with evident satisfaction when I told him of my evening's adventures.

Gourgaud told me that, under Napoleon's directions, he had written a full account of the Waterloo campaign, but that it had never been finished, as Napoleon could never decide upon the best way of ending the great battle; that he, Gourgaud, had suggested no less than six different ways, but none were satisfactory.

His animosity to Montholon was violent, and he vowed that, should they ever meet in Europe, he would call him to account. After close questioning, I could not elicit that there had ever been adequate cause for this enmity, but was led to think that it arose from jealousy of Montholon's sway over Napoleon's household, and of the favour in which he stood.

To finish about Gourgaud, I may add that on his reaching England, after one or two interviews with the Under Secretary of State, he fell into the hands of certain Radicals of note, who represented to him the folly of his conduct in turning against Napoleon; that as his adherent he was really somebody, whereas he was only ruining himself by appearing as inimical. In short, they so worked upon the poor weak man, that he was induced to try and make it appear that he was still *l'homme de l'Empereur*; this he did by inditing a letter to Marie Louise, in which he inveighed against the treatment of Napoleon at the hands of Government and Sir Hudson Lowe, which being duly published, Gourgaud fell to zero in the opinion of all right-minded persons.

The immediate consequence was, that Government arrested him, and sent him out of the country in charge of a police constable, by virtue of the Alien Act then in force. He was taken to Hamburg, where he got into pecuniary difficulties; in his distress he applied to Madame de Montholon, who, having left St Helena, was then residing at Brussels, and she, still despising the man, sent him a hundred *louis d'or*. Eventually he returned to France, where, in his own opinion, he became a man of some note, married money, or, as he expressed it, *fit un mariage de convenance*, drove a *tilburie anglaise*, and dressed in the height of Parisian fashion; but what most surprised me, was to learn from the

Montholons, that he had become *un homme raisonnable*; moreover, and to my astonishment, I learned they were actually on visiting terms with their St Helena arch-enemy.

In order to account for my knowledge of these little matters, as well as of others that the reader will come to, I ought to mention my having visited Paris in 1828, and, when strolling on the *Boulevards*, met Montholon, who invited my wife and self to pass a few days at his Château de Frémigny. Being very desirous to have some talk with him about St Helena, when all reserve on his part might be dispensed with, I accepted the friendly proposal.

On arrival, we found Frémigny to be a charming country house, standing in extensive grounds. There were other visitors besides ourselves, all, save a French officer, being English. The Count's horses and carriages were also from England, as was his valet; in short, he seemed possessed with Anglomania. Our stay became prolonged, and I had a good deal of conversation with both host and hostess, upon matters of interest, relating to St Helena. He enlarged upon what he termed *la politique de Longwood*, spoke not unkindly of Sir Hudson Lowe, allowing he had a difficult task to execute, since *an angel from Heaven as Governor could not have pleased them.*

When I more than hinted, that nothing could justify detraction and departure from truth in carrying out a policy, he merely shrugged his shoulders, and reiterated, "*C'était notre politique, et que voulez-vous?*" That he and the others respected Sir Hudson Lowe, I had not the shadow of a doubt; nay, in a conversation with Montholon at St Helena, when speaking of the Governor, he observed that Sir Hudson was an officer who would always have distinguished employment, as all Governments were glad of the services of a man of his calibre.

Happening to mention that, owing to his inability to find an officer who could understand and speak French, the Governor was disposed to employ me as orderly officer at Longwood, Montholon said it was well for me that I was not appointed to the post, as they did not want a person in that capacity who could understand them, "In fact," he said, "we should have found means to get rid of you, and perhaps ruined you." Now, it was [so decided] simply because an officer of the rank of captain had always acted at Longwood, and the Governor knew that to have sent them an officer who was only a lieutenant, would have been deemed a kind of insult by Napoleon, and as such resented.

I was subsequently glad the project failed, when I came to see all the difficulties incident to an employment which could not possibly be satisfactory to the officer, since he was in a manner responsible for the captive's safety, without having the means of being certain of it, as I knew that for weeks together the patient orderly officer, though constantly prowling about the house, never got a glimpse of Napoleon. I can only therefore surmise that Government felt that the position of the island, the nature of its coasts, and the well-considered precautions of our watchful Governor, precluded the possibility of evasion, notwithstanding Gourgaud's assertions to Baron Stürmer.[6]

---

6. There is plenty of evidence that the British Government knew of plans of escape, and took them seriously. Whether any were really feasible or not, is another question. See especially a plan of escape described by Dr. J. H. Rose in his essay "Napoleon's Detention at St. Helena," p. 510, of *Owen's College Historical Essays*, recently published. Sir Hudson Lowe's conduct shows that the official rules were never relaxed until quite a late period of the captivity.

CHAPTER 14

Conclusion

But I must think of bringing my recollections to a close, and fear I have already tired the reader's patience—Indeed, he has to thank me for cutting out many pages; still, I must beg to trespass a little longer upon it, as I could wish those who may not have fallen in with Mr Forsyth's excellent and important work,[1] to become better acquainted with the true character and conduct of Sir Hudson Lowe, so different from the pictures which odious calumny and downright lying have put forth. Perhaps I could not do better than extract portions of Mr Forsyth's preface, with this object.

> When his vast pile of papers was committed to me by Mr Murray,[2] I was not asked to make out a case for Sir Hudson Lowe, nor, had I been asked to do so, would I have consented. I regarded the duty of examining the papers left by him as a solemn trust, for the due and truthful discharge of which I was responsible to the public, and a still more searching tribunal, my own conscience: *Amicus Socrates, amicus Plato, sed magis arnica Veritas.*. .
>
> As to the style and manner in which I have performed the task, it is not for me to judge. That question will be decided by the

---

1. A French gentleman—a Bonapartist—to whom I lent this book, told me, after reading it, that it satisfied him Sir Hudson Lowe had been a much injured man.— "History of the Captivity of Napoleon at St Helena; from the letters and journals of the late Lieut.-Gen, Sir Hudson Lowe, and official documents not before made public. By William Forsyth, M.A. In three volumes. John Murray, Albemarle Street, 1853."

2. The words, "When his vast pile of papers was committed to me by Mr Murray," are not a verbal quotation, but give the effect of the preceding sentences. The verbal quotation begins, "I was not asked . . ."

public for themselves, and every writer must submit himself to their impartial opinion, from which there is no appeal. But I do claim for myself the right to be believed, when I assert that the present volumes have been written with the most minute and scrupulous regard to truth.

If the language in which I have frequently spoken of O'Meara seems severe, let the reader, before it is condemned, consider whether it has not been deserved. I am not one of those who think that such conduct as he has been guilty of in slandering others may be sufficiently censured in the dulcet tones of gentle animadversion. He merits a sterner and more fearless judgement. Such writers are the pests of literature. They corrupt the stream of history by poisoning its fountains, and the effect of his work has been to mislead all succeeding authors, and perpetuate a tale of falsehood.

As regards Napoleon, if I know anything of myself, my sympathies were in his favour. I cannot now sufficiently express my admiration of his genius; but neither can I blind myself to the fact that he did not exhibit in misfortune that magnanimity without which there is no real greatness, and that he concentrated the energies of his mighty intellect on the ignoble task of insulting the Governor of St Helena, and manufacturing a case of hardship and oppression for himself. I have endeavoured to hold the balance even, and it is not the weight of prejudice, but of facts, which has made one of the scales preponderate.

It will be to me a source of sincere and lasting satisfaction if I have, with the most rigid adherence to truth, and by the mere force of facts, succeeded in vindicating the memory of those who have been long calumniated, and proving that neither the British Government nor Sir Hudson Lowe was in fault as regards the treatment of Napoleon at St Helena.[3]

Let me now say a few words respecting the materials I have used. And here I cannot do better than quote the late Sir Hudson Lowe's own account of the papers in his possession, which he drew up when he contemplated a publication of them in his lifetime—a design, however, which, unfortunately for his reputation, he failed to execute. He says, 'There are perhaps few, if

---

3. This paragraph concludes Forsyth's preface. The next paragraph immediately follows that ending with the word "preponderate." Then comes a long gap before the concluding paragraph.

any, public administrations of any kind, of which the records are so full and complete as those of my government at St Helena. There is not only a detailed correspondence addressed to the proper department of His Majesty's Government, reporting the occurrences of almost every day during the five years that Napoleon Bonaparte remained under my custody, but the greater part of the conversations held with Bonaparte himself, or with his followers, was immediately noted down with an ability and exactness which reflect the highest credit on my military secretary [Major Gorrequer].

This gentleman was not only a perfect master of the French language, but possessed a memory equally remarkable for its accuracy and tenacity, and was therefore eminently qualified to report the conversations at which he was himself present, and to detect any error to which a misapprehension of the meaning of foreigners might lead other persons who repeated what passed at interviews with Bonaparte and his followers.'

I think it was a great mistake to allow of Mr Barry O'Meara becoming Napoleon's medical adviser, and another great mistake was in not stipulating that, as such, he should be subject to the same restrictions as the French gentlemen of his suite. Without his assistance the great captive and his attendants could have caused comparatively little trouble and anxiety; whereas Mr O'Meara was able to go about as he pleased, was able to obtain full information as to all measures taken for Napoleon's safe keeping, could correspond with England, and in many other ways serve the objects of his immediate master.

All this would not have been prejudicial had he been true to his salt; but I *know* that was fully enlisted for Napoleon's service during the voyage from Rochefort to England. Being a man of some tact and ability, he contrived for a good while to keep on good terms with Sir Hudson Lowe, who was pleased to learn how things went on at Longwood, never suspecting that a British officer, a surgeon in our Navy, could be disloyal. At length suspicion arose, and proof was obtained of his aiding in a secret correspondence, when the Governor, of course, shut him up in Longwood, and shortly after sent him to the Cape of Good Hope, whence he sailed for England.[4] He then addressed a long

---

4. The actual dismissal of O'Meara from St Helena was in consequence of orders from Government (see *Forsyth*, 3, 47). He was sent direct to England, sailing from St Helena by H.M. sloop *Griffon*, 2nd August 1818.

letter to the Admiralty, full of abuse of Sir Hudson Lowe, but overshot the mark by more than insinuating that the Governor desired the death of his captive. This passage in his letter ran thus:

On some of these occasions he [the Governor] made to me observations upon the benefit which would result to Europe from the death of Napoleon Bonaparte, of which event he spoke in a manner which, considering his situation and mine, was peculiarly distressing to me.

The reply from the Admiralty was as follows:—

It is impossible to doubt the meaning which this passage was intended to convey, and my Lords can as little doubt that the insinuation is a calumnious falsehood; but if it were true, and if so horrible a suggestion were made to you directly or indirectly, it was your bounden duty not to have lost a moment in communicating it to the Admiral on the spot, or to the Secretary of State, or to their Lordships.

An overture so monstrous in itself, and so deeply involving not merely the personal character of the Governor, but the honour of the nation and the important interests committed to his charge, should not have been preserved in your own breast for two years, to be produced at last, not (as it would appear) from a sense of public duty, but in furtherance of your personal hostility against the Governor.

Either the charge is in the last degree false and calumnious, or you can have no possible excuse for having hitherto suppressed it.

In either case, and without adverting to the general tenor of your conduct as stated in your letter, my Lords consider you to be an improper person to continue in His Majesty's service, and they have directed your name to be erased from the list of naval surgeons accordingly.

The late Dr Walter Henry, who at St Helena was assistant-surgeon to the 66th Regiment, and afterwards rose to a high position in the medical staff of the army, with whom I was intimate at the island, and who was a personal friend of O'Meara, until he lost his character, thus writes in his interesting and amusing volumes: [5]—

5. *Events of a Military Life: being Recollections after Service in the Peninsular War, Invasion of France, the East Indies, St Helena, Canada, and Elsewhere.* Pickering, London, 2nd edition, 1843.

I have been informed since, on authority which I cannot doubt, that Mr O'Meara had a friend in London, the private secretary of Lord M——,[6] who found it convenient to have a correspondent in St Helena, then a highly interesting spot, who should give him all the gossip of the island for the First Lord of the Admiralty, to be sported in a higher circle afterwards for the Prince Regent's amusement. The patronage of Lord M—— was thus secured; and Mr O'Meara, confident in this backing, stood out stiffly against Sir Hudson Lowe. The latter was quite ignorant of this intrigue against the proper exercise of his authority; and when he discovered it afterwards, he found it was a delicate matter to meddle with, involving the conduct of a Cabinet Minister, and affecting, possibly, the harmony of the Ministry. Even after the development of the vile poisoning charge against the Governor, the influence of the First Lord was exerted to screen O'Meara, but in vain; for Lord Liverpool exclaimed, as in another well-known instance, of a very different description, 'It is too bad!'

Still Mr O'Meara has had his reward. He is now beyond the reach of praise or blame, but it Can scarcely be deemed harsh or uncharitable to say, that his conduct at St Helena made him very popular with the Liberal section of politicians. He has been embalmed in a couplet by Lord Byron, was pensioned deservedly by the Bonaparte family, admitted to the affections of a rich old lady on account of his politics, and again largely pensioned by his doting wife; besides being admired, quoted, and panegyrised by all Bonapartists yet extant, all the Levellers, Jacobins, and Radicals, and a large proportion of the Democrats and Republicans in the world.[7]

It behoves me now to say somewhat about what Montholon terms the *politique* of Longwood. When Napoleon came to take a survey of his position at St Helena, and of political circumstances in Europe, he early made up his mind that the sole possibility of his ever leaving the island rested on the remote prospect of a change in British public opinion regarding him. In our Parliament, certain influential members of the opposition had censured Government for so unworthily treating an exiled sovereign, who had cast himself upon British hospitality; and, as a drowning man catches at a straw, he deluded himself with the

6. Lord Melville, then First Lord of the Admiralty.
7. Henry, 2, 43 foll.

idea that these persons were really his friends, instead of seizing the truth that their declamation was simply to annoy their opponents.

The policy of Longwood— heartily and assiduously carried out by his adherents, who liked banishment as little as the great man himself—was to pour into England pamphlets and letters complaining of unnecessary restrictions, insults from the Governor, scarcity of provisions, miserable accommodation, insalubrity of climate, and a host of other grievances, but chiefly levelled at the Governor as the "head and front" of all that was amiss.

Certainly Longwood House[8] could hardly be deemed a suitable residence for so important a captive, and provisions may not have been of the highest quality, although the best the island afforded, but no others of the complaints were valid. As to the house, it offered the only situation calculated to insure security, a paramount object, and which Sir G. Cockburn kept in view when seeking a proper place of residence. Let me here mention that, from whatever cause, Napoleon had taken a great dislike to the Admiral, and this was flagrantly shown by grossly insulting him. It happened in this wise: the Admiral and Governor went together to Longwood, in order for the latter to be presented to the illustrious exile.

On the door of the audience room being opened, the Governor's name was called, and he stepped forward; but when the Admiral advanced, a servant placed his arm across the doorway, and kept him back.[9] This insulting and undignified proceeding on the part of Napoleon was never generally known until Gourgaud left, when he told me of it, adding that both he and the other French generals felt shocked and ashamed that such an insult should have been offered to a British Admiral.

But, *pour revenir à nos moutons*, so well did the Longwood clique, including Mr O'Meara, take their measures, hesitating at no vituperation or falsehood to further their ends, that they so far succeeded as to cast a heavy slur on the Governor, both in England and France; they ransacked history for prototypes of him, and discovered them in the execrable Gournay and Mautravers, the murderers of Edward the Second; nay, as we have seen, O'Meara denounced him to the Admi-

---

8. Longwood was about the only house from which escape was difficult. Plantation House was the centre of the semaphores of the island, and was therefore expressly reserved by the East India Company to be the residence of the Governor.
9. There is no evidence that this was done by order of Napoleon. In fact, he afterwards sent his apolosies to the Admiral.—See *Forsythe*, 1, 143.

ralty as having spoken to him of the advantage that would accrue to Europe at large if Napoleon were disposed oft

This reads truly farcical, but shows the fiendish nature of the Longwood conspirators, although its absurdity must strike any person of reflection, considering that Sir Hudson Lowe, a young major-general, was holding a most important office, with a very large salary, and was consequently deeply interested in prolonging so honourable and lucrative an employment, even putting out of sight all moral consideration.

As may well be imagined, I felt curious to glean a knowledge of Napoleon's habits, thoughts, and opinions, etc., and, situated as I was, there was no lack of opportunities, as the reader will see, when I mention that not only did my duties bring me into contact with most of the French, but for a considerable time I lived in a cottage on the confines of Longwood Park, and messed with the orderly officer, and the surgeon attached to the establishment (Dr Verling, Royal Artillery). Hence I was, so to say, living under the same roof with the Montholons, and, indeed, with Napoleon himself. Having plenty of time at my disposal, and being always well received by the Count and Countess, I scrupled not to visit them daily, and seek to profit from intercourse with persons of their cultivated minds; moreover, this enabled me to improve my French, for although I could speak it with facility, my knowledge of it was far from perfect.

It will readily be conceived that the intimacy which thus arose tended in a great measure to lessen reserve, and that I was treated as a kind of *ami de la maison*. Then it must also be borne in mind that at Frémigny the talk about Napoleon was naturally more free than at St Helena. In the following meagre remarks jotted down, some learned at Frémigny, others at Longwood, it will be seen that several bear relation to the period when he was in power.

He could not tolerate persons who were independent of him; therefore disliked the wealthy, whilst he revered *la noblesse*.

It was a necessity in him to say unpleasant things to persons about him, and to disparage merit.

Mistrustful and on his guard with all who approached him—apt to talk too much, and then to *recourir après*, or seek to undo what he had said.

Ignorant on many subjects, but readily acquiring a knowledge of anything worth treasuring.

Of a good disposition naturally—had much feeling—desiring affection, though doing his best to defeat such object.

Timid by nature—hence his want of ease when in company.

Constantly seeking to entrap persons, but deceiving nobody by his dissimulation.

Could bear no obstacle to his will, or contradiction, but ready to welcome truth if well *motivée*.

Flattery failed towards him; probity and diligence succeeded, because they served his interests; whereas flattery only touched his passions, and those he sacrificed to his interests.

Immorality *le froissait*—the memoirs of Madame d'Epinay were distasteful to him.

An organised system of *espionnage* existed in his household, and he ever sought to set its members at variance, in which he was only too successful.

Wanted good manners, from not seeing good society in early life.

Often used coarse and vulgar expressions, as calling people *f——bêtes*, etc.

Thought much of his personal appearance—anxious to learn what people said of his *physique*.

Fond of teasing (*laquinerie*).

Absence of dignity in his deportment and manner. "*Il lui manquait d'être né sur le trône.*"

Thought with precision, but was diffuse in expressing his thoughts, having a poor command of words, though fancying himself master of the French language, which was not the case.

Could not have friends, for he loved no one, and frequently inflicted mortal wounds on the *amour propre* of others.

For his ministers he often selected mediocrity rather than talent, lest his projects should be penetrated.

With his servants at times too familiar—at others capricious and violent, administering *coups de poing*.

He had no religion—was a materialist.

Talking with a lady of rank and wit, whose father had been a *fermier général* of the revenue, he asked if she remembered what Mezeray says about *fermiers généraux?* "Yes," she replied, "and I also remember what he says of *parvenus.*" We may feel sure that, if true, it occurred before he wore the imperial purple.

As to his daily habits at the island, there is little to be said. He rose late, partook of a slight breakfast; often passed hours together in a tepid bath, read after his manner, which was to glance over a page *avec le pouce,* thus getting through two or three volumes in less than as many hours; dined early, usually alone, and very abstemiously, drinking a little claret and water; had a horrid habit of spitting, and when lying in bed would indulge it without regard as to where the *crachat* might fall, whether on bed-curtains or carpet. All stood in his presence, and when on his deathbed, poor Antommarchi (his doctor) was kept standing until ready to faint;[10] slept badly, and, as we have seen, would have Montholon often roused out of bed for dictation. That Napoleon had moral courage in the highest degree is certain, but it is equally certain that he had not the kind of courage which prompted Gustavus Adolphus to rush into the midst of the fight at Lützen, or, like the hero of Trafalgar, to make himself a mark for the foe by appearing in the battle decorated with *stars* and *orders*. Most assuredly, it is seldom the duty of a commander-in-chief to expose himself in the van, but occasions will arise when personal danger should not be considered. For his fame, Napoleon ought to have headed the Imperial Guard in the last onset at Waterloo; but he forgot what he told his army when about to cross the frontier—that the time had arrived when every brave Frenchman should conquer or die!

Were I inclined to swell out these pages, I might do so by recounting how, after entire approval of Sir Hudson Lowe's conduct during a very onerous and important duty by Government, neither any considerable employment nor pension was granted to him—and how, in his *Life of Napoleon.* Sir Walter Scott did him injustice; how he returned from Ceylon, in order to publish a refutation of the injustice, but was dissuaded by Lord Bathurst; [11] and how the Duke of Wellington rose in the House of Peers in his vindication. All, however, is afforded us by Mr Forsyth; and, moreover, I must bear in mind that few persons are deeply interested, like myself, in the memory of Sir Hudson Lowe.

I have in my possession some letters, written to me by Sir Harris

10. So in Lady Malcolm's *Diary of St Helena,* p. 43, we read of Admiral Malcolm: "He was four hours with him (Napoleon); they walked all the time in the drawing-room with their hats under their arms."

11. What Lord Bathurst disapproved of was not Sir Hudson Lowe's defending himself in writing, but his returning from Ceylon in order to do so. Previously he had written to Sir Hudson Lowe in a letter dated 28th November 1823: "I have always thought that whatever might have been the result of your late proceedings [*i.e.* against O'Meara for libel] you owed it to yourself, after all that had been said against you, to draw up a full and complete vindication of the administration of your government at St Helena, coupled with all the documents in your statement. It will be for consideration when it will be prudent to publish it." (See *Forsyth*, 3, 323 and 331.

Nicolas, when he was engaged in sifting Sir Hudson's papers, having been entrusted with them by Mr Murray, of Albemarle Street, but who died before the work he was preparing had advanced very far. I cull from them a couple of extracts, which are valuable as being from the pen of an impartial writer:—

Boulogne,
14th March 1848.

You will be glad to know, that the memoirs of Sir Hudson Lowe are in the press, and that I am perfectly satisfied with the result of the St Helena investigation. Not a spot will, I hope and believe, rest upon his memory, and such an exposure of *lying*, *malignity*, and scoundrelism on the part of O'Meara, Montholon, Las Cases, Antommarchi, etc., as the work will exhibit, will be almost unprecedented. You will perceive that I have given *every document* of the slightest interest, and I have pointed out every lie that has been uttered, so far as my proofs extend.

Boulogne,
30th March 1848.

Your remarks on St Helena are more important than you can be aware of, because they bear on many points in which I wished for additional evidence. I wish I had read them before the article on Montholon in the next *Quarterly* was written; however, I shall use them strongly in the work. I feel very sensibly indeed the kind manner in which you aid me. and it is very probable that I shall often trouble you. Mr Murray speaks of his having seen you, and is much obliged for your attention. By the time I have finished, I think I shall have been in company with *more liars* than any living author. My God! if people meet in the next world with a knowledge of each other, and with an exposure of their several falsehoods and villainy, what must have been the scenes between Sir Hudson, Las Cases, and O'Meara!

It might have been expected that the death of Sir Hudson Lowe would have put a stop, and forever, to the vituperation which pursued him to the grave. Within the last few months, however, the *St James's Magazine* published a series of papers, purporting to be written by a man of the name of Stewart, who pretended to have been a confidential servant of Napoleon at Longwood. I read the papers, and can aver that no such person was *so* employed, that is, *confidentially*. In fact, the man's statements are a tissue of ridiculous falsehoods from beginning to end. The name of Sir Thomas Reade,[12] who was at the head of the St Helena Staff, also comes in for a share of abuse. His son, our consul at Cadiz, wrote me on the subject, and also to the late Admiral Rous. Here is the Admiral's reply:—

13 Berkeley Square,
22nd July 1876.

Dear Sir,—The account of Napoleon at St Helena in the *St James's Magazine* is a tissue of falsehoods. In page 249 of the June number, I am reported to have been present at an altercation between the author and Sir T. Reade, and to have given Mr Stewart two dollars. I never knew Mr Stewart, and I left St Helena in June 1819, having commanded H. M. S. *Podargus* on the station from April 1817.

I state, upon my honour, that I do not believe either Sir Hudson Lowe or Sir Thomas Reade was capable of performing any act derogatory to the character of a gentleman. To the best of my knowledge all reports of ill-treatment to Napoleon were systematic falsehoods, fabricated with a view of keeping alive a sympathy in Europe to enable his friends to succeed in obtaining a more agreeable exile.—

I am, yours truly,
H. J. Rous.

The insertion of this letter recalls to my memory our St Helena racing, over which Captain Rous ruled with all the authority he so long exercised at Newmarket. We had our Turf Club, and an excellent mile-and-a-half course at Dead wood. It is true that our horses were not of high quality, but they afforded quite as much amusement as if they had been thoroughbred Rous infected me with his racing taste, and he found me an apt pupil, though invariably opposed to him. The Governor was very liberal in his patronage, giving two handsome plates annually, and generally attended the sport in person; he also placed his horses at the command of Captain Rous, and as they, or some of them, were English, and the best in the island, he enjoyed great advantages. The light weights of both army and navy furnished jockeys, and all turned out in proper racing equipment.

Garrison races always afford fun and amusement, but I shall not dwell upon those of the island; one trifling incident, however, oc-

12. Sir Thomas Reade was an officer who distinguished himself by valuable service in the Mediterranean, for which he received the honour of knighthood.

curred, which shows the value of blustering when it is judiciously used. Rous had entered his Admiral's horse, by name Slamby, to run in a handicap race with several others; well, Slamby and another came in together, and almost everybody thought it a "dead-heat." Not so Rous; he rushed towards the stand of the stewards, vociferating, "Slamby has won, I'll bet a thousand pounds." This took effect with the stewards, who announced Slamby as winner; Rous then said aside to me, "If that was not a dead-heat, I never saw one." So much for the excitement of racing, coupled with anxiety to gratify his Admiral!

Although so long Nestor of the English turf, I do not suppose the Admiral ever appeared as a jockey at home, but at St Helena he did on one occasion so exhibit himself. More than once he spoke to me of riding himself, but being a fine man, over six feet, I think, I never expected to see him ride. However, he proposed a match between an animal of mine and a strong English horse which a friend lent him for the purpose, he and I to be the jockeys, which was accepted, and he turned out faultless in dress from top to toe. As we rode together to the starting-post, I found he had misgivings as to the result of the race, and he said he hoped I would bring him in handsomely—that is, not win by too great a distance. I won it, as I expected, but think he bore me a grudge ever after for not bringing him in handsomely enough; in fact, I was afraid of making it a close thing.

Dr Henry, whom I have already had occasion to quote, relates the following incident, which I well remember:—

During the first day's sport after our arrival, an awkward circumstance occurred on the course, which everybody regretted when it could not be helped. A certain half-mad and drunken *piqueur* of Napoleon, named Archambault, took it into his head to gallop within the ropes when the course was cleared, and the horses coming up. For this transgression he was pursued by one of the stewards, and horse-whipped out of the forbidden limits. This gentleman knew not that the offender belonged to the Longwood establishment, or he would, no doubt, have spared his whip—particularly as Napoleon at the time was sitting on a bench outside his residence, looking at the crowd through a glass, and we were apprehensive that he might interpret the accidental chastisement his servant had received, into a premeditated insult to the master.

But we did Napoleon injustice by the supposition. Mr O'Meara told me the next day, that he had distinctly witnessed everything that passed, and had been very angry when he saw Archambault galloping alone along the course, and was pleased to see him chastised; and that he had called him into his presence, and expended on him a few *f—— bêtes* and *sacré cochons*, afterwards.[13]

Having opened Dr Henry's book, I am inclined to take more extracts, to show that the island is not the wretched barren rock which its libellers have described it to be, nor unhealthy, but, on the contrary, very salubrious.

There is a wooded mountain ridge in St Helena, called Diana's Peak, three thousand feet above the level of the sea, from which the view is wonderfully grant! and vast. The eye commands the whole island, with a circle of three or four hundred miles of ocean, until the distant horizon mingles with the sky. This is a celebrated spot for picnics, although the labour of clambering to the top is no trifling undertaking for a lady; and the narrow ledge, or back-bone, at the summit affords but a very nervous promenade. The whole mountain is covered with the *Geoffrœa*, or cabbage-tree, shaped exactly like a large umbrella. Under this dense shade enormous ferns arise, some eighteen or twenty feet in height; but here, as all over the island, there is a dearth of wild flowers. . . . The rides on the highlands generally were remarkably agreeable; the air was cool, the road good, and every turn or fresh elevation presented some new and striking combination of picturesque objects.

The road running round Diana's Peak to Sandy Bay Ridge was a general favourite, as it afforded at almost every step the most wild and extraordinary prospects. On attaining the top of the ridge, a scene of singular sublimity expands at once, looking quite unearthly, and like a bit of some strange planet at first, until the old association with our own globe is renewed, by the names of two rocky obelisks standing boldly out of the vast hollow. These are called Lot and his wife; for the uncanonical people here have made a pillar of the gentleman as well as the lady. Sandy Bay is seen to windward, in the distance, with its line of white surf; and here and there a pretty patch of cultivation strikes the eye, ttiched in some sheltered nook; fantastic, peaked, and splintered mountains rise all around, and beyond

---

13. Henry, 2, 26.

St. James' Bay from Ladder Hill

all appears the illimitable ocean, with the cruising vessels, like white specks upon its surface, perhaps stretching out to arrest the course of some strange ship coming right down on our island.[14]

Then as regards salubrity, here is Dr Henry's statement:—

For a tropical climate, only 15° from the Line, St Helena is certainly a healthy island, if not the most healthy of this description in the world. During one period of twelve months, we did not lose one man by disease out of 500 of the 66th, quartered at Deadwood. In 1817-18-19 Fahrenheit's thermometer, kept at the hospital there, ranged from 55° to 70°, with the exception of two calm days, when it rose to 80°. It was about 12° higher in the valleys and in James Town on an average; but from the situation of the latter, and the peculiar radiation of heat to which it was exposed, the temperature was sometimes upwards of 90°. The great source of health and comparative coolness in St Helena is the south-east trade wind, coming from an immense extent of the Southern Ocean, which winnows the rock, and wafts over it every morning a cloudy awning that mitigates the strong sun. This is not without concomitant humidity in the highlands for half the year; but the inconvenience is as nothing compared with the comfort, fertility, and salubrity which the clouds bestow.

Notwithstanding the assertions of Napoleon's adherents, who had an interest in painting the place in as dark colours as they could, I must maintain that, correctly speaking, we had no endemic disease in the island. Human life, certainly, did not extend to the same length as in cooler regions, though some organs appeared to be privileged there: diseases of the lungs, for instance, being very rare. It has been stated that there are no old people in the island, but this is certainly a mistake, though the proportion may appear small to an English eye. I believe it is as large as in Spain and the south of Italy; and I have seen some blacks of eighty, and whites approaching ninety. The upper parts of St Helena, including the residence of Bonaparte, are decidedly the most healthy; and we often moved our regimental convalescents from James Town to Deadwood for cooler and better air. The clouds moved so steadily and regularly with the

14. Henry, 2, 62, 63.

trade wind, that there appeared to be no time for atmospherical accumulations of electricity, and we never had any thunder or lightning. No instance of hydrophobia in man or any inferior animal had ever been known in St Helena.[15]

Amongst a people like the French, who have thrown off all worship save that of *la Gloire*, there can scarcely be a doubt that Napoleon will go down to their posterity as the "Great," a title which writers of history have rarely awarded to any but wholesale spoliators and shedders of torrents of blood—the scourges of mankind. I was about to let my pen run on, and presumptuously dwell a little upon the character of Napoleon, but bethought me in time of the valuable maxim, so often overlooked, *Ne sutor ultra crepidam*; besides, we have only to turn to the pages of Mr Forsyth, to find it depicted with equal truth and eloquence:—

"If Napoleon," says that writer,[16] "behaved in exile with the dignity and fortitude which his worshippers pretend, and Sir Hudson Lowe's conduct was such as they ascribe to him, then indeed the Governor was the tyrant, and the prisoner the victim. But the very reverse of this was the case. Napoleon outraged Sir Hudson Lowe with every species of insult. His constant habit was to speak of him in epithets which no gentleman can hear applied to himself without his blood tingling in his veins. His object throughout seems to have been to provoke and foster a quarrel, in hopes of having some tangible cause of offence to complain of. We have seen that he expressed disappointment and vexation that he could not make the Governor angry. The imperturbable temper of the latter, imperturbable at least towards his prisoner, was a rock against which the wave of his passion expended itself in vain.

"That brain, on whose tissues at one time hung the diplomacy of Europe, busied itself at St Helena in schemes of which the immediate purpose was to mortify and annoy Sir Hudson Lowe. On one occasion, when by a stratagem of Montholon he obtained a copy of a note addressed by the Governor to the Marquis de Monchenu, he was, we are told, joyful as on a day of victory. Alas! how was the mighty fallen! His complaints of ill-treatment were loud but insincere, and were dictated, not by

---

15. Henry, 2, 45, 46.
16. *Forsythe*, 3, 306 foll.

The room in which Napoleon died. As it appeared in 1850

suffering, but by policy. I do not believe that Napoleon seriously contemplated as a possibility clandestine escape, for no man had a clearer or more just discernment when decision was necessary, and he knew that his island prison was too well guarded to render any plan of evasion practicable. But he never ceased to cherish the hope that he would be allowed to return to Europe. He thought a change of ministry in England might effect this, for, ignorant of the latitude of attack in which political parties amongst ourselves indulge, he naturally built much upon the language of the Opposition. If Lord Holland became Prime Minister, it seemed an inevitable consequence that Napoleon must be free.

"But interest in his fate might die away if it were not kept alive by sympathy and compassion. If he declared himself satisfied with his treatment, there would be little to expect from the zeal of partisans in his behalf. 'At one time,' says Sir Hudson Lowe, 'I had hoped that I might help him to support his great reverse of fortune, but I soon discovered that his first and strongest wish was to aggravate and heighten the grievances of his situation, and that the greatest unkindness I could be guilty of was to leave him no cause of complaint.' Therefore it was that the cry of suffering arose at St Helena, and was carried across the Atlantic, to be echoed by rumour with her thousand tongues, until men began really to believe that the illustrious prisoner was treated with causeless and disgraceful severity.

"No one can study the character of Napoleon without being struck by one prevailing feature,—his intense selfishness. This was caused partly, no doubt, by the unparalleled success which had for twenty years attended his career, and which made him look upon himself as a being born under a star, and as one whose destiny it was to rule, while it was the destiny of others to obey. Under the chariot-wheels of his ambition he was ready to crush everything that opposed his path, without compunction or remorse. He regarded others merely as instruments to be used by him, and to be flung aside when he had no longer occasion for them.

"A memorable example of this occurs in his treatment of the noble-minded Josephine. Because she gave no promise of an heir to the throne, he snapped the cord of affection in a moment. The ties of duty and of love were nothing in his eyes

117

when he found that his wish for a son was not likely to be gratified. How little feeling did he show when he heard of the death on the battle-field of any of the generals and marshals to whom he seemed to be most attached! Indeed, as has been already mentioned, he said of himself that his soul was of marble, and it was thus insensible to some of the finest feelings of our nature. Not that Napoleon was without gentleness and even playfulness in his disposition. When pleased and unopposed, there was a charming vivacity in his manner which irresistibly won all hearts. He was fond of *espièglerie* even with grown-up people, and in the case of children, who were always favourites with him, there was no limit to his good humour. But he could not brook contradiction or opposition, and had not the slightest consideration for others when they stood in the way of his caprice. He was the sun round which others were to revolve, but, though attracted by his influence, they were kept at too great a distance to feel the warmth of his friendship or affection. Each of them might say with Helena:—

In his bright radiance and collateral light
Must I be comforted, not in his sphere.

"Another feature in the character of Bonaparte which must not be lost sight of, and which has an important bearing upon the question of his treatment at St Helena, was his habitual disregard of truth. His moral sense was so blunted that he had no scruple in resorting to deceit, and, if necessary, to falsehood, if he could thereby accomplish an object in view. It has been said of him by a French writer, with sarcastic severity (Jules Maurel), that he was in the *Moniteur* the first journalist of the Empire, and that he kept what he won with his pen much longer than what he won with his sword. He here gave himself an unbounded licence of invention, and made events assume whatever complexion he pleased, taking care that it was such as harmonised with his projects, and flattered the vanity of the French nation. It was thus that the victories of Wellington in the Peninsula were ignored; and after terrible reverses, France was told that the English would have been crushed by Napoleon, if he had thought that the proper moment for the catastrophe had arrived.

"At St Helena he gave full scope to this propensity. The letters which he there dictated to his obsequious followers, and which have made such an impression on the public mind, are filled with glaring misstatements of facts. They may be called the bulletins of his exile, which were intended to deceive the people of Europe, as the bulletins of his battles were intended to deceive the French. Even Bertrand was ashamed of them, and more than once disowned the responsibility of their authorship, although he submitted to the humiliation of writing them, and subscribed them with his name.

"'That monologue of six years,' says Lamartine,[17] 'which he addressed to the world from the summit of his rock, and the most trivial words of which were registered by his courtiers to be transmitted to his myrmidons as the gospel of party, was nothing more than a long diplomatic note, void of good faith, addressed to his partisans, and speaking in turns the language of all the factions that he wished to nourish with his memory, instead of being the disinterested, sincere, and religious effusion of a soul which bequeaths, with its greatness, its failings, its truth, and its repentance to the world.'

"Can we then be so infatuated with hero-worship, so dazzled by the splendour of intellectual gifts, as to allow ourselves to treat gently and speak lightly of this contempt of veracity, this disdain of the first and simplest requirement of the moral law? No more pernicious lesson can be taught than the doctrine that success, which elevates a man to the pinnacle of power, absolves him from the obligation to observe the imperishable distinction between right and wrong. And we do in effect teach that doctrine when we forbear to censure in Napoleon Bonaparte a want of truth, which we should condemn in another as a meanness and a disgrace.

"When we turn from his character to his actions, and ask in what respect he benefited mankind, the answer is most unsatisfactory. Perhaps no man ever, for the sake of his own restless ambition, inflicted so much positive misery upon his species. His path was that of the destroyer. Kingdoms were trodden down under the iron heel of conquest, and wherever he appeared with his armies, blood was poured upon the ground like water. A fierce soldiery was let loose upon the countries of Europe, which spoiled the inhabitants, ravaged the fields, and

17. In his *Histoire de la Restauration*, 6, 408.

swept away, as with a whirlwind, the accumulations of years of Industry and peace. A military despotism on a scale of unparalleled magnitude was established, which abrogated all political rights, and strove to trample out all national distinctions. If the sorrows of a single hero or heroine in a talc of fiction can move our hearts and powerfully awake our sympathies, let us think for a moment on the amount of human suffering caused by the career of Napoleon.

"It is hardly an exaggeration to say that the land was as the Garden of Eden before him. and behind him a desolate wilderness. Tears did not fail to flow for each homestead burned, each family outraged, each peasant and each soldier slain, in that long series of years during which he ruled the destinies of France. And what did France gain under his sway? A code of laws which is his best title to her gratitude, and that which she values more—military glory. But at what a price was that glory purchased! The bravest and the best of her sons died in distant fields of battle, amidst the sands of Egypt, or the snows of Russia. A ruthless conscription depopulated the villages, and at last reached, in its downward course, youths who were just emerging into manhood, but who were still rather boys than men. Her treasure was exhausted, her liberties were gone. A system of *espionnage* betrayed family secrets to the minister of police, whose agents were everywhere, and whose omnipresence no one could escape. And at last came bitter retribution for the long-continued and daring attempt against the rights of nations. Her soil was invaded, her capital was taken; and Pandours and Cossacks bivouacked in the Champ de Mars, while English soldiers kept guard at the Louvre, and foreign bayonets brought back the King whom she had driven into exile and proclaimed an outlaw.

"Of his merits as a great captain we need not speak. Such a world-conqueror will perhaps never be seen again. But we may hope the time is coming, if, indeed, it has not already come, when men will sit in stern judgment upon those who, without adequate and just cause, and for the sake of their own aggrandizement, involve nations in strife. War is in itself an unmitigated curse. It is indeed the abomination of desolation. It may impose upon the imagination with all its proud pomp and circumstance, and few sights can be conceived of more thrilling interest than the march of a great army in compact array. But follow that army to the battlefield. See it after the shock of conflict, when the clash of swords is over and the artillery has ceased to thunder. Listen to the cries of the wounded and the groans of the dying: follow the surgeon, and observe what *his* mission is when the battle is won, and acres of God's fair earth are strewed with corpses and converted into a vast charnel house.

"And what sorrow accompanies the tidings of every victory! The child is fatherless, and the wife a widow, and the wail of mourning for those who have fallen mingles with the shout with which the nation exults in its success. War may be a necessity in defence of outraged rights, and to repel aggression, but it ought ever to be looked upon as a miserable calamity, and he who wantonly provokes it is one of the worst enemies of his race. No man ever felt this more strongly than Wellington. No great commander was more anxious to avert the horrors of war. He said that the most dreadful thing next to a battle lost was a battle won; and it is one of his best titles to the gratitude of Europe that he always fought for peace.

"But who can say this of Napoleon? His whole public life was one series of acts of hostile aggression, and we do not find it recorded that he ever betrayed compunction or expressed remorse for the loss of the countless thousands whom his ambition caused to perish by the cannon and the sword."

I may here just allude to a few of the numerous publications that appeared from time to time for the purpose of keeping alive an interest in Europe about Napoleon. The first that reached us did not, however, emanate from Longwood, neither could it be surmised there who was its author. It was entitled *Manuscrit de Ste Hélène*,[18] purporting to give the opinions of Napoleon on a variety of subjects, but—so far as I can recollect—making no complaints of his treatment on the island. It was cleverly written, and evidently by a man conversant with public affairs in France.

This gave rise to a small volume written by Montholon, entitled *Manuscrit de l'Ile d'Elbe*,[19] which combated some of the propositions

---

18. The full title is *Manuscrit venu de Ste Hélène d'une maniere inconnue*, London, 1817. This book is generally attributed to M. Lullin de Chateauvienx.

19. I can find no trace of this book, and doubt its existence. Montholon was not with Napoleon at Elba, and in any case it is a strange title for an answer to anything from St Helena.

Napoleon's Tomb

stated in the *Manuscrit de Ste Hélène*, but I remember little about it. and was not struck by the ability of the writer. I think it did not dwell on the grievances of Longwood.

A pamphlet was published by an inferior servant of Longwood, named Santini, who left for Europe; for what cause I do not recollect. I have no doubt that it was written for him; he was an ignorant man.[20]

Immediately on reaching England, Las Cases put forth a pamphlet. On its receipt at Longwood, Montholon read to me the opening chapter; and a good laugh we had at the ridiculous vanity of the little man in describing his family as of higher antiquity than that of the King of France. Of course it was full of complaints of his master's unworthy treatment in exile.

His rather voluminous journal appeared as soon as it could undergo revision and sundry additions; for, when printed, it differed in many respects from the manuscript which he carried home.[21]

Some of these passages are quoted by Forsyth.

The most virulent publication was Mr O'Meara's *Voice from St Helena*, in which he strove to avenge his "ill-treatment" by the Governor, and was penned with an affected candour that had its effect on the public mind.

One or two little pamphlets, which I have forgotten, and occasional letters in *opposition* newspapers, served to keep Napoleon before the public.

Meanwhile, nothing appeared on the *per contra* side but a short pamphlet, of little account, from the pen of Mr Theodore Hook, who passed a few weeks at St Helena when on his way home from the Mauritius, where he had been treasurer, and where he was seized with what he termed a "complaint in his chest." The pamphlet was entitled "Facts illustrative of the Treatment of Napoleon in St Helena." But, though powerful in fiction, "facts" were quite out of his province; at all events, we did not think much of "Theodore's facts," though written with a praiseworthy intention, and [yet], looking at the numerous publications emanating from Longwood, Hook's facts remind us of

---

20. This pamphlet was really written by Colonel Maceroni, an officer who had served under Murat.

21. In Las Cases' journal, as published, several passages in the manuscript are suppressed. When Las Cases was arrested at Longwood, Sir Hudson Lowe had the manuscript of his journal copied, and a copy of the passages suppressed is now in the British Museum among the Lowe papers.

the "one halfpenny worth of bread to an intolerable deal of sack."

I forget how many volumes were published by Montholon in after years, entitled *Mémoires pour servir à l'Histoire de France*—I think some seven or eight; one or two purported to be written by Las Cases, the Waterloo one by Gourgaud, and one, I think, by Bertrand; all, however, were revised and published by Montholon, as I was informed.[22]

I have reason to believe that no portion of those volumes was dictated by Napoleon with greater self-gratification than the lengthy chapter entitled "*Mariage de l'Empereur.*" The reader may plainly see how proud he was of espousing a daughter of the House of Hapsburg. In truth, his tendencies were purely aristocratic. I well remember being told at St Helena of the extreme annoyance he felt when some ship captain who caught a glimpse of him at Longwood, described him, in a published letter, as wearing round his head a red kerchief; "*Comment*," said he, "*on me fait porter le bonnet rouge!*"

My principal object in writing about St Helena is to justify Sir Hudson Lowe, and I think that if I append a few extracts from his private journal and notes, my readers will see that he was no ordinary man. His military career was one of extraordinary activity and success, exhibiting wonderful energy and remarkable ability. He entered the army in 1787; was a captain in command of a levy, styled the Corsican Rangers, in 1795 stationed at Minorca.

The Corsican Rangers formed part of the expedition to Egypt, landing and being warmly engaged on the 8th March 1800 [1801], and sustaining in several conflicts heavy loss. The regiment was present at the battle of Alexandria, and Major Lowe received the first proposals for the surrender of Cairo. His zeal and ability in command of the outposts, on various occasions, obtained for him this flattering encomium from General Moore: "Lowe, when you're at the outposts, I always feel sure of a good night's rest." And the same gallant and distinguished officer, when writing [27th October 1801] to Major Lowe's father, thus spoke of his son:—

> In Sir Ralph Abercrombie he lost, in common with many others, a good friend; but, however, his conduct has been so conspicuously good, that I hope he will meet with the reward he merits.

---

22. The author seems here to be confusing these *Mémoires pour servir* by Montholon and Gourgaud with the *Recueil de pièces authentiques sur le captif de Sainte Hélène* to which many, including Las Cases, Gourgaud, Bertrand and Montholon, contributed.

Sir Robert Wilson, writing of the campaign,[23] says of the Corsican Rangers, "This corps in every action, and especially in the landing, distinguished itself particularly; and Major Lowe, who commanded it, gained always the highest approbation. Indeed, it was a corps which, from its conduct and appearance, excited general admiration, and did honour to the nation of the First Consul of France."

At the Peace of Amiens, this corps was disbanded, and Major Lowe was placed on half-pay; but was soon afterwards appointed to the 7th Royal Fusiliers. Congratulating him upon this appointment, General Moore wrote [21st April 1802], "It is nothing more than you well deserve, and if I have been at all instrumental in bringing it about, I shall think the better of myself for it. . . . I trust you will always consider me as a person warmly interested in your welfare."

In 1803. Major Lowe was appointed one of the permanent assistant quartermaster-generals at home. "If," wrote Sir John Moore [15th June 1803], "I have had the good fortune to get you employed in the way you wish, I am glad of it. I have known you a long time, and I am confident your conduct, in whatever situation you are placed, will be such as to do honour to those who have recommended you."

At this time, Major Lowe was sent on a secret mission to Portugal, for the purpose of ascertaining the military condition and resources of that country, in the districts of Oporto. Viaña, Valença, Chaves, Bragança, and Almeida. Having carefully inspected these places, he reported favourably of the troops and defences, and expressed an opinion of the practicability of defending the country by united British and Portuguese means. Immediately afterwards he was sent to the Mediterranean to raise another corps of Royal Corsican Rangers, of which he was appointed lieutenant-colonel.

After much difficulty, he succeeded in raising his regiment, which formed part of Sir John Craig's expedition to Naples; and Lieutenant-Colonel Lowe commanded the advance of the army, but the troops returned to Sicily *re infectâ*.

The island of Capri having been captured, Colonel Lowe, with part of his regiment, was sent to garrison it [June 1806]. When the island was attacked by an overwhelming French force,[24] the little garrison made a gallant defence during sixteen days, when the town was evacuated, and the garrison marched out with all the honours of war

---

23. In his *History of the British Expedition to Egypt.*
24. The numbers were; Garrison, 1362 (of whom 700, Maltese troops, were untrustworthy); French assailants, at least 3000.

[October 1808].

Colonel Lowe and his regiment next took part in an expedition to the Bay of Naples under Sir John Stuart, but soon returned to Sicily, and shortly after joined an expedition under Brigadier-General Oswald, which drove the French from the islands of Cephalonia, Zante, Ithaca, and Cerigo [October 1809]. The first division, under Colonel Lowe, disembarked at Zante. Cephalonia was next attacked, and taken. "I have," says General Oswald in his despatch, "nominated Lieutenant-Colonel Lowe to the important duty of commanding this island, certain that so delicate a trust could not be reposed in more able hands."

Yielding to Colonel Lowe's opinion, General Oswald attacked Santa Maura, when Colonel Lowe greatly distinguished himself, and the island became the presidency of a Government, comprising the Islands of Cephalonia and Ithaca. In announcing this appointment, General Oswald said he was confident "that it would be most grateful to the Government and population of Cephalonia and Ithaca, to know that they would still enjoy the benefits arising from the civil administration of an officer who had shown himself the common father of all ranks and classes of these communities." Here Colonel Lowe remained for [nearly] two years.[25]

In January 1812, he obtained the rank of full colonel, after twenty-four years of very active service; and in January of the following year was sent to the north of Germany, to inspect a body of troops raised by the authority of the Emperor of Russia, and named the "Russian-German Legion." Landing at Stockholm, he had interviews with the King and Queen and Crown Prince of Sweden, and met the celebrated Madame de Staël and her daughter. Madame de Staël had fitted up a little theatre in her house, and she and her daughter went through some of the finest scenes in Racine's tragedy of *Iphigénie*. The performance was admirable, The appearance of Bernadotte (the Prince Royal) greatly struck Colonel Lowe.

"I have never seen," he wrote, "so remarkable a countenance as that of Bernadotte; an aquiline nose of most extraordinary dimension, eyes full of fire, a penetrating look, with a countenance darker than that of any Spaniard, and hair so black that the portrait painters can find no tint dark enough to give its right hue; it forms a vast bushy protuberance round his head;

---

25. From April 1810 to February 1812. On his departure the inhabitants of these islands presented Colonel Lowe with a gold sword, accompanied by an address of thanks.

and he takes great pains, I understand, to have it arranged in proper form."

Colonel Lowe joined the headquarters of the Emperor of Russia at Kalisch, in Poland, and the Emperor informed him that the corps of which he was in pursuit, was between Narva and Königsberg, scattered over an extent of five hundred miles. After performing the duty of inspection, Colonel Lowe was an eyewitness of the hard-fought battle of Bautzen [20th and 21st May 1813].

In July, he was directed to inspect the whole of the levies in British pay in the north of Germany, amounting to nearly twenty thousand men; for which laborious duty he got no remuneration.

In October, he was attached to the allied Russian and Prussian army under the command of General Blücher. and was with him in every action in which he was engaged from the battles of Möckern and Leipsic, until the surrender of Paris. He was present at the general actions of Brienne, La Rothière, Champaubert, Méry, Craone, Laon. Fère-Champenoise, and Paris; forming in all, including Bautzen, Wurschen, Möckern and Leipsic, thirteen actions, in eleven of which the enemy's army was commanded by Napoleon in person. He was privy to many important deliberations, in which, as the only British officer of any rank employed with Blücher's army, he was able to offer suggestions upon measures influencing the fate of the war, particularly during the time of the conferences at Châtillon, when he strongly and eagerly advised the march against the French capital, as the only means by which the power of Bonaparte could be overthrown, and a solid peace obtained.

When the capital of France was entered by the allied armies, Colonel Lowe brought the news of Napoleon's abdication to England. He was immediately knighted by the Prince Regent; the Prussian Order of Military Merit was soon after conferred upon him, as also the Order of Saint George from the Emperor of Russia. These were accompanied by very gratifying letters. His promotion to the rank of Major-General followed, and he was appointed Quarter-master-General to the British troops in the Low Countries. In May 1815, he was offered the command of a division of British troops at Genoa, which was landed at Marseilles early in June.

The following letter [dated 23rd November 1814] received by Sir Hudson, when at Brussels, from the Prussian General Count Gneisenau, bears such honourable testimony to the merits of Sir Hudson Lowe, that I am induced to give it *in extenso*:—

It is with great satisfaction, my very dear and honoured General, that I have received your letter of the 15th of September, which tells me that you have still preserved the remembrance of a man who is infinitely attached to you. and who in the course of a memorable campaign, if there ever were one, has learnt to appreciate your rare military talents, your profound judgement on the great operations of war, and your imperturbable *sang froid* in the day of battle. These rare qualities and your honourable character will link me to you eternally. You may always pride yourself. General, on having belonged to the small number of those who opposed to timid counsels a firmness not to be shaken by the reverses we sustained; and you have never departed from the conviction that to bring Europe back to a just and equitable equilibrium, and to overthrow the Government of Imperial Jacobinism, its capital ought to be seized. Without that there is no safety. Happily the event has justified your calculations. . . . Your appointment,[26] my dear General, must place you in continual relation with the Duke of Wellington.

You would oblige me infinitely by being the medium of presenting to that hero the sentiments of respectful homage which I feel for him. By the circumspection with which he conducted the war in the Peninsula, he prepared and led to that state of things which enabled Europe to emancipate herself; and it was after his fine campaign against Masséna, that they began in Russia to believe in the possibility of resistance, and commenced making preparation for it. Grateful posterity will count the Duke of Wellington among the benefactors of the human race.[27]

In 1825, Sir Hudson Lowe was appointed to the command of the troops at Ceylon, and, as the "Eastern Question" was even then one of moment in the Councils of Europe, he resolved to go out by the overland route, which few up to that time had tried. Sir Hudson's object was to see as much as he could of Turkey, and form his own opinions of its defences. On reaching Vienna, he was surprised to learn that the Emperor Alexander, having heard of his proposed route, had sent instructions to his minister at Vienna, and at other places, not only to

---

26. As Quartermaster-General to the British troops in the Low Countries.
27. This letter also appears in *Forsyth*, 1, 110. The original is in French. See also other correspondence between General Gneisenau and Sir Hudson Lowe, published by Dr J. H. Rose in the *English Historical Review* for July 1901.

furnish him with the necessary passports for travelling through any part of the Russian dominions, but had given directions also that he should be received with the highest military honours wherever he passed. This would have probably led him to take the route of the Black Sea, Georgia, and Persia, but a very few days afterwards the news arrived of the Emperor Alexander's death: he, therefore, resolved on pursuing the route he had at first intended, *viz.*, by Egypt and the Red Sea.

"I went," wrote Sir H. Lowe, "from Vienna through Hungary and Transylvania, and across the noble frontier of the Carpathian mountains, to Wallachia. Here I found an Austrian minister established, but no Russian or accredited agent for any other European Power. From Wallachia I crossed the Danube, which was at that time frozen over and covered with snow; in fact. I was riding across the river without being aware that I was upon it, until the banks were pointed out by my guide, which circumstance I have here mentioned as a proof that the river, although there are no bridges over it, offers no good frontier, as an army with all its train of carriages might have passed over any part with facility between the fortresses at that time.

"I then crossed the Balkans, which appeared to me not to present so good a line of frontier as the Carpathian mountains, but still a very defined and a very noble one, presenting commanding positions at almost every turn of the road. I passed also the position of Shumla, which I examined with some care, knowing it had been the scene of contest in former wars. Upon my arrival at Constantinople, I learnt that Sir Stratford Canning, who had been just then appointed to the embassy, had not arrived there, being wind-bound at Gallipoli. He arrived, however, shortly afterwards, when I pointed out to him the route I intended to take in proceeding to Egypt. I mentioned my intention to visit the Dardanelles, or rather the position of the Chersonesus, which forms the right bank of the strait of the Hellespont, and was most readily and obligingly furnished with every necessary passport for the prosecution of my journey.

"Having hired a small vessel to take me from Constantinople to the Dardanelles. I landed at Gallipoli, and had every opportunity I could desire for visiting that point and its neighbourhood. I crossed the Strait to Abydos, afterwards travelled over the plain of Troy and through part of Asia Minor to Smyrna, from which

I embarked for Egypt in the *Zebra* sloop of war."

All the observations and suggestions of Sir Hudson Lowe were duly sent to Lord Bathurst for the information of the Cabinet, and were subsequently printed, along with much other matter having relation to the East, for private circulation.

Sir Hudson went to Ceylon with the understanding that he should succeed to the government of that island eventually; but when the vacancy next occurred there had been a change of Ministry at home, and he met with a cruel disappointment.[29]

I think that those of my friends to whom I shall send copies of my little publication, will now be of opinion that I may take a pride in having been honoured with the regard of Sir Hudson Lowe.

---

29. The next vacancy occurred near the end of 1830, a short time after Earl Grey had become Prime Minister.